SHAKESPEARE, PERFORMANCE AND THE ARCHIVE

Shakespeare, Performance and the Archive is a movingly written exploration of what remains when actors evacuate the space and time of performance. An analysis of "leftovers," it moves between tracking the politics of what is consciously archived and the politics of visible and invisible theatrical labor to trace the persistence of performance.

In this fascinating volume, Hodgdon moves away from reconstructing a theatrical past in favor of considering how documents, material objects, sketches, drawings and photographs do work that is neither strictly archival nor documentary but performative—that is, they serve as sites of re-performance. *Shakespeare, Performance and the Archive* creates a deeply materialized historiography of performance and attempts to make that history do something entirely new.

Barbara Hodgdon is Professor of English at the University of Michigan, now retired. Her major interest is in theatrical performances, especially performed Shakespeare. She is the author of *The End Crowns All*, *The Shakespeare Trade* and most recently the Arden 3 edition of *The Taming of the Shrew*.

SHAKESPEARE, PERFORMANCE AND THE ARCHIVE

Barbara Hodgdon

Routledge
Taylor & Francis Group

LONDON AND NEW YORK

First published 2016
by Routledge
2 Park Square, Milton Park, Abingdon, Oxon OX14 4RN

and by Routledge
711 Third Avenue, New York, NY 10017

Routledge is an imprint of the Taylor & Francis Group, an informa business

British Library Cataloguing-in-Publication Data
A catalogue record for this book is available from the British Library

Library of Congress Cataloguing-in-Publication Data
Hodgdon, Barbara, 1932–
Shakespeare, performance and the archive / Barbara Hodgdon.
pages cm
Includes bibliographical references and index.
Shakespeare, William, 1564–1616—Dramatic production. I. Title.
PR3091.H56 2015
792.9'5—dc23
2015018319

ISBN: 978-0-415-68295-4 (hbk)
ISBN: 978-0-415-68296-1 (pbk)
ISBN: 978-0-203-14445-9 (ebk)

Typeset in Bembo
by Swales & Willis Ltd, Exeter, Devon, UK

Printed and bound by CPI Group (UK) Ltd, Croydon, CR0 4YY

To Richard Abel, without whom . . .
And that's that, said Pooh. What do we do next?

CONTENTS

FIGURES

Chapter 3

Chapter 4

Epilogue

ACKNOWLEDGEMENTS

First of all, a triumvirate of Presences. Deep thanks to Laurence Burns for his photographs. His artistry, and especially his fashioned collaboration with Peter Brook, make this study possible. Deep thanks also to Richard Abel, for showing me how to look and to read a photograph. And to Antony Sher, for graciously permitting Richard and me to photograph pages from his rehearsal scripts and granting permission to reproduce his self-portrait as Lear's Fool. Thanks also to Ian McKellen and Harriet Walter, for so willingly granting permission to include rehearsal script pages. Crucial figures at various archives have made working there a distinct pleasure: Biddy Hayward, curator of Laurence Burns' archive; Helen Hargest, Madeleine Cox and Paul Taylor at the Shakespeare Birthplace Trust; Roger Howells, the Royal Shakespeare Company's "unofficial" historian; David Howells for showing off the RSC's Collections and providing access; Kate Dorney, Chief Curator of the Victoria and Albert Theatre and Performance Archive; Laurence Ward and David Payne at London Metropolitan Authority; Kate Hutchens and Rachel Baron Singer, very special Special Collections Librarians at the University of Michigan. Several individuals, both in England and the States, have been there from the beginnings, when this project was something else entirely: Carol Chillington Rutter of the University of Warwick, with me every step of the way, and William Ingram at Michigan, for sharing what he knows and showing me where to find precisely the citation or image that I didn't know I wanted until it proved to be there. And others: Sally Jacobs, for granting permission to include her sketch of David Waller as Bottom; and for great talk and encouraging words, Robert Shaughnessy at the University of Kent, Michael Cordner and Tom Cornford at the University of York, Peter Holland at the University of Notre Dame and Bill Worthen at Columbia University and Barnard College. Particular thanks to Mike Schoenfeldt, Chair of English at Michigan, for permissions funding. And to Rabbit's Friends and Relations—Kentston Bauman, Amy Rodgers,

Stephen Spiess, Katie Will and Asynith Palmer, all former doctoral students in English at the University of Michigan who made teaching and mentoring so memorable. Finally, I have been especially fortunate that Talia Rodgers at Routledge wanted the book (and waited so patiently for it) and that Harriet Affleck, Kate Reeves and Rachel Singleton, her colleagues at Routledge, have so carefully shepherded it through production.

INTRODUCTION

The lure of leftovers

1978: Spring in Stratford, rehearsals for John Barton's *Love's Labour's Lost*. On one morning, designated for work on the Nine Worthies' Show, the giant hobby-horses—leftovers from Barton's 1972 *Richard II*—graze comfortably in the upstage park of the Conference Hall. Costard (Alan Hendrick) gallops in on a small wooden horse, while a trio made up of Dull (David Lyon) on drum, the Forester (Dennis Clinton) on horn and cymbals and Jacquenetta (Ruby Wax) on tambourine accompany him, backed up with improvised toots, drum rolls, clangs and horse-hoof sound effects made with two wooden blocks, all supplied by Stephen Dobbin, the Deputy Stage Manager. Sir Nathaniel (David Suchet), surprisingly and completely encased in one of the huge horses, only part of his nose and mouth visible in his oversize helmet, is the next Worthy: carrying a fifteen-foot pennant lance and an enormous shield (a *Troilus and Cressida* leftover), he cuts an impressive figure, yet one glance at the audience of courtiers makes him dry in his role; his voice straining into a soprano register, he begins to sink ever so slowly into the floor, horse and all, shield askew, lance descending. The room rocks with laughter. "You must be careful," Barton remarks, "these horses can upstage a man."[1] Suchet, over lunch: "Do you think he'll let me keep it in?"

As an observer of that rehearsal process, I recorded the company's day-to-day explorations, their working conversations. My log documented anecdotes, signs of thought occurring inside and outside the rehearsal room; voices of actors, directors, stage managers, my own—a bricolage, a chorus of voices. Performance "survives as a cluster of narratives"—everyone in that rehearsal room had a different story.[2] When, ten years later, I wrote about that experience, my aim was to privilege process over product. Now, however, as I look back at what I wrote, it seems unusually text-tied, a chronicle of how the text was made to perform. Looking back, I also see how that essay engages my obsession with archiving photographs of performances as mnemonics of what occurred—trying to find shots where "the energy of the stage work continues glowing in a supposedly 'still' image" that carries a sense of spontaneity, a touch of theatrical accident or coincidence.[3] I'm drawn to these, likening them to a drawing or cartoon, a "thinking still"[4]—what text does not or cannot say often emerges in a photo. The photo constitutes "the visible remains of what is no longer visible, a fragment that steals theatre, stills it—and dis-stills it"— it is the primal leftover and the one I tend to accord pride of place.[5] Like an author's working draft or an artist's cartoon, rehearsal offers a preliminary array of aesthetic theatrical decisions—many of which elude performance.

This book could be called a collector's history, though that phrase doesn't quite encompass the "stuff" that's here—especially photographs but also anecdotes (the marginal made symbolically central) and analects—selected miscellaneous written passages. It also depends, in part, on what's absent—for instance, the chosen photographs that are here stand in for others that, for one reason or another, could not be acquired or reproduced and so must be accounted for by deep description. Just as archaeology is "about writing around what is obstinately not there," writing about performance and performance-in-process depends on a semiotics of absence, and results in constructing a performance-about-performance—a second-order performance, one which stages a reintegration of surviving fragments.[6]

To unpack my own archive (with thanks to Walter Benjamin),[7] I open a catch-all cupboard's doors where file cabinets filled with folders containing theatre programs, theatre photographs and postcard sets from specific performances reside: being freed from the file drawer's darkness and brought into the light signifies their rebirth, their renewal. Touchstones of theatre-going, they constitute a record of ownership—a way of saving (stealing?) performance. Also surviving in that cupboard—my private wonder cabinet—is a freekah left over from Peter Brook's 1970 *Midsummer Night's Dream*: a performance piece with many guises, including a sneaky snake or a mirror for Bottom-as-an-ass. "To see is to have at a distance," writes Merleau-Ponty, embedding the idea of ownership in the idea of seeing— which Benjamin expands in his formulation of aura—"a strange weave of space and time, the unique appearance or semblance of distance, no matter how close it may be" and, more expansively: "Ownership is the most intimate relationship one can have to objects. Not that they come alive in him; it is he who lives in them."[8] At a remove from historical and cultural context, they are redefined in terms of the collector as archivist.[9]

The earliest known archives contained objects neatly strung up on suspended threads, "one thing after another," which functioned as navigational tools, allowing users to keep their bearings in time and space, much like Ariadne's thread helped Theseus navigate his way through Daedalus' labyrinth.[10] Benjamin writes: "We go forward, but in so doing, we not only discover the twists and turns of the cave, but also enjoy this pleasure of discovery against the background of the other, rhythmic bliss of unwinding the thread."[11] In rehearsal scripts, for instance, doing so resembles pulling a string through the notations, crossing and criss-crossing them, isolating narrative threads that connect one page to another, adding grammatical

FIGURE 0.1 Freekah. Author's collection. Photograph © Richard Abel.

insertions such as parentheses, slashes, brackets and arrows—props that emphasize or connect one context to another.

This archive, then, is concerned with the persistence of rehearsal as and of performance. As in archaeology, rehearsal has to do with cues or prompts of site, with signs, traces, sources and documents: excavating such materials and bringing them to the surface invites viewing psychoanalysis as an archaeology of the psyche.[12] Like performance, rehearsal survives as "a cluster of narratives": both are deeply concerned with "retrieval, recording and reassembling";[13] both also are theoretically grounded in poaching or raiding—interdisciplinary borrowing and appropriation, a flexible, fluctuating discourse of remains. Waking from his dream, Bottom's senses have gone awry—"The eye of man hath not heard, the ear of man hath not seen, man's hand is not able to taste, his tongue to conceive, nor his heart to report, what my dream was." Whereas Bottom has the inimitable Peter Quince near at hand to write a ballad of his dream, my ballad of being-ness or present-ness, of embodied mind and en-minded body, burrs onto this Bottom-esque world, where seeing and hearing are sharpened, and given the materiality of the photograph, where seeing punctures saying.[14]

In choosing photographs, I look for those that will, someday, provide fodder for an essay or book—though until recently this book was not specifically what I had in mind. My archive also includes step-by-step accounts of some performances, expansive at times, at others rather mundane (and then this or that happened): at best, these descriptions work to celebrate theatrical lives lived—those of actors, directors, photographers (especially Laurence Burns), stage managers, deputy stage managers, observers and spectators—all who have a hand in creating, shaping and interpreting performance. A few questions thought about, addressed (or not). How does one particular photograph—Titania asleep with Bottom on a red feather, Oberon and Puck on trapezes, waiting to waken her, for instance—come to stand for a performance and seemingly blur out or erase any and all other images?[15] Or, as a polar opposite, consider shots that belie either rehearsal or performance—most poster images or, in a unique instance, Alan Howard's self-designed photo of himself in his dressing room, surrounded by objects crucial to a world tour and constructed for a particular audience, his fans: the space of the shot is the only place where that performance occurs. And one more: Antony Sher's trick of animating his rehearsal script with drawings of himself and fellow players, a document decorated or redesigned with a novel form of marginalia. What's here ranges from shots of performance; readings from production notes, publicity leaflets, press releases, reviews and training exercises; materials from personal notebooks; anecdotes about their genesis; remembered excerpts from Q&A sessions with various audiences; memories of performers and witnesses alike, colored by nostalgia and hindsight; scribbles on ever-smaller pieces of paper, indecipherable notes written on coffee-stained post-its; fragments, sounds and thoughts remembered when waking and as quickly forgotten. When gathered together, such scraps, scribbles, drawings and fragments might be called an object biography that reflects on performance processes, explores their historical density. The model for this work, oddly enough, was my so-called Memory Book—a document I inherited from my mother, its materials for memory celebrating events from birth announcements, first shoes, school photographs, shots of birthday parties, pressed corsages from long-ago dances, diary fantasies about the names (Jay Holahan, who was tall and could waltz) on those dance cards. An object prized for its power to carry the past into the future, this was an upscale version of my earliest, short-lived archive of material remains: birds' nests, empty locust skeletons, dried flowers marking the seasons.

A guitar, a harp, a few cushions, several discarded cloaks scatter-framing a white space of *Dream*'s stage: a tableau of what remains—objects and costumes— once actors have vacated the space and time of live performance[16] that gestures directly toward the archive, searching through legacies left as endowments in public or boxed away in private archives. To situate myself in relation to this gathering of material evidence is to write a history that, as Carolyn Steedman writes, "gives a habitation and a name" to all the fragments and traces—"all the inchoate stuff,"[17] and especially to selected remains—that have ended up in the archive. Inevitably, such a history begins with naming names—of archives and collections. All the archives I've consulted to collect my own wonder cabinet of leftover remains are British: the Shakespeare Birthplace Trust; Shakespeare Centre Library, which houses the collected photographs of Joe Cocks and Tom Holte, Stratford photographers; Royal Shakespeare Company Archives; British Library; Victoria and Albert Theatre and Performance Archive; National Theatre Archive; London Metropolitan Archive; the Chapter of Southwark Cathedral; Ian McKellen's Archive (held at the Victoria and Albert Theatre and Performance Archive); Antony Sher's personal archive (private); Miriam Gilbert's Theatre Diaries (also private); and Laurence Burns' Photographic Archive, managed by Biddy Hayward. Materials from the Royal Shakespeare Company Archives, the

National Theatre Archives, the English Shakespeare Company Archives and Laurence Burns' photographs most firmly anchor my study.

In addition to citing these locations, there is more to the story of how I started collecting photographs. Beginning in the early 1980s, I selected shots from Joe Cocks' Stratford shop, trawling through contact sheets of performances I had seen, choosing photographs that would serve as mnemonics of striking moments of performance. Whether consciously or unconsciously, I imagined that this collection would provide fodder for an essay or book: though this particular book was far in the future, I also had a specific model—and a specific photographer—in mind. In 1989, memories of the ending of Michael Bogdanov's *Romeo and Juliet* prompted an essay—"Absent Bodies, Present Voices: Performance Work and the Close of *Romeo and Juliet*'s Golden Story"[18]—which reproduced Laurence Burns' photograph of that ending. By 2008, in the midst of editing *The Taming of the Shrew* for the Arden 3 series, I wrote to Burns, asking to publish yet another image of ending—Paola Dionisotti's Kate kneeling to Jonathan Pryce's Petruchio. Attached to the photograph was a note explaining that Dionisotti wearing Kate's cap was a mistake, and this began a conversation—was it really a mistake or was the mistake a surprise that gave the shot a cluster of meanings?—that still continues, circulating around his photographs for both *Wars of the Roses* and *Dream* as well as his memories of crafting them. For Burns photographs not just rehearsal and performance—process and product—but also "the act of looking itself": his "performed photography"[19] constitutes one way of looking, figuring a conflation of photography, choreography and the body's time. As I write, I am moved and dictated to by photographs chosen by Burns himself, though I also have chosen some images from contact sheets. As always, research is a fortuitous process: situating myself means imagining a fiction of that process. Even photographs have limits: I remain mindful that the images at hand cannot restore, as if by magic, what is lacking in every gaze.[20] They do, however, reveal something about the nature of perception within the spatial architecture of the stage space and the physical structure of light. Significantly, the rehearsal photograph is the image par excellence of looking at performance in reverse, of generating the illusion that spectators are not looking. Someone is always looking, but the rehearsal shot pretends that this is not the case. Is it, perhaps, even more performative than the performance itself?

Looking at leftovers moves from tracking the poetics of what is consciously kept, saved and archived, and the visible and invisible theatrical labor brought to bear on those remains in order to trace the force of performance. Although Peggy Phelan's claim that performance becomes itself through disappearance haunts these pages, my study continues the work I've been doing—with a difference. Here, I shift from considering performance as product to focusing on performance as process, drawing on memories (mine as well as those of others), photographs, actors' annotated rehearsal scripts and rehearsal notes, prompt scripts, prop scenarios and costumes—materials already collected as well as new ones which potentially give access to scenarios of action and behavior, to the embodied practices toward which these remains gesture, where context sutures them, each to each. In doing so, I construct a time capsule that explores liminal territory, the marginal zone between rehearsal and live event; rehearsal offers an experience analogous to that of meeting with the writing that precedes performance, echoing its memory-work in another register. In short, the leftovers that fascinate me are not indexical signs of a theatrical past; rather, the work they do is neither strictly archival nor documentary but performative—sites of re-performance for which I together with other readers constitute a present audience. Breaking down divisions between spectator and actor, acknowledging that both play *act-ive* roles, I borrow Augusto Boal's legendary term, "spect-actor," a participant engaged in re-imagining and re-animating performance.[21]

The story I'm telling accounts for the shift from words to images, a transformation that relies on and emphasizes bodies, draws upon fleshly memories. With those bodies in mind, this is a kind of detective story with an occasionally forensic cast. One context for this collection of materials informing practice deciphers traces left by what is no longer extant, signaling their rebirth, their renewal, as dreamwork—that is, it forges connections in an indefinite, historically dense network.[22] A "happy disorder," writes Benjamin, who grounds his methodology on literary montage: "I needn't say anything. Merely show … the rags, the refuse—these I will not inventory but allow to come into their own: by making use of them."[23] Photographs, however, do not describe in the same way as writing nor do they share the same temporality as text. It often requires annotations to give images a voice.[24] Story-telling as visual historiography? More strictly, it resembles an archaeological reading, especially in terms of the performance of presence in analyses of the trace, the record, the memory, the document.[25] Since photography and performance obviously inform each other—both, notes Phelan, are rooted in the metaphor of the copy—photographs track across this study. In selecting shots for this image-driven account, I have chosen to think synchronically and/or thematically, especially when taking up rehearsal photographs. After all, rehearsals do not necessarily take place chronologically or in narrative order until the process comes close to run-throughs (if then). Not only do the promptscript's erasures and over-writings, which parallel rehearsal's times and timings, bear witness to echoes and/or changes, but each chapter also reads photographs through a slightly different lens.[26]

This study, then, falls into four chapters and a catch-all epilogue that looks to the future. Chapter One—"Material Remains at Play"—integrates an analysis of several photographs with marginalia which track the step-by-gesture construction of character—in this case, Ian McKellen's portrayal of Richard III—through various "backstage" documents, primarily though not exclusively dresser's notes. Chapter Two—"Rehearsal Remains or Reading From the Margins: Actors' Scripts"—considers annotated scripts by Ellen Terry, Ian McKellen, Harriet Walter and Antony Sher. Engaging with those annotations, I talk back to these actors' readings and (beyond them, tacitly) to Shakespeare. To push this idea further is to say that each script is a paper stage that brings a fleeting assemblage of voices into visibility, unsettling expectations of singular meanings. Chapter Three—"Storytelling, Anecdotes,

Ethnography: The ESC's *Wars of the Roses*"—focuses on Michael Bogdanov and Michael Pennington's epic venture, staging and touring a history cycle over four years (1986–1989)—with a difference, in that it seeks to reanimate Laurence Burns' photographic record of their ambitious project of traveling world-wide, what I've called Theatre-In-Transit. Chapter Four—"Dreaming in the Archives"—moves to explore Laurence Burns' tranche of rehearsal photographs for Peter Brook's legendary 1970 production of *Midsummer Night's Dream*, tracing how they anticipate a narrative of performance as well as paying particular attention to Burns' photographic artistry.

These photographs can be thought of as images stored in memory, which is not an inventory but an *act*—call it a performance?—of memorizing, theatre resonating with archaeology. Theatrical stills preserve moments of rehearsal and/or performance times, fragments of bright moments, preventing them from being effaced by the supersession of the next phase or phrase. John Berger writes, "Whereas remembered images are the *residue* of continuous experience or consciousness, a photograph isolates the appearances of a disconnected instant."[27] Working much like the classical means of remembering by placing a thought or image within a fictive theatrical architecture,[28] the still braids production technologies with modes of performance to thematize a hyperframe, a master code for re-dreaming rehearsal as well as performance.[29]

Notes

1 See Barbara Hodgdon, "Rehearsal Process as Critical Practice: John Barton's 1978 *Love's Labour's Lost*," *Theatre History Studies* (January 1, 1988), 29–30.

2 Stories from watchers and watched and those who mediate between the two positions: there is no single overriding authority—see Mike Pearson and Michael Shanks, *Theatre/Archaeology* (London: Routledge, 2001), 53, 57–59.

3 Laurence Burns, cited in Barbara Hodgdon, "Photography, Theater, Mnemonics; Or, Thirteen Ways of Looking at a Still," in *Theorizing Practice: Redefining Theatre History*, eds. W.B. Worthen with Peter Holland (London: Palgrave Macmillan, 2003), 93, 94.

4 For the thought behind the "thinking still," see Roland Barthes, *Camera Lucida: Reflections on Photography*, trans. Richard Howard (New York: Hill and Wang, 1981).

5 For the idea of a theatrical unconscious, Rosalind E. Krauss, *The Optical Unconscious* (Cambridge, MA and London: MIT Press, 1993), 179.

6 Pearson and Shanks, *Theatre/Archaeology*, 60, 65.

7 Walter Benjamin, "Unpacking My Library: A Talk About Book Collecting," in *Selected Writings*. vol. 2, part 2, 1931–1934, ed. Michael W. Jennings et al. (Cambridge, MA: Belknap Press of Harvard University Press, 1999), 486–493.

8 Benjamin, "Unpacking My Library," citing Merleau-Ponty, 67. For aura, see "Little History of Photography," in *Selected Writings*, 518.

9 Susan M. Pearce labels this fetish collecting. See *On Collecting: An Investigation into Collecting in the European Tradition* (London and New York: Routledge, 1995). See Janet Staiger, "Cabinets of Transgression: Collecting and Arranging Hollywood Images" *Participations* vol. 1, Issue 3 (February 2005), 7 for Pearce's three schemas. Michael Camille views collecting as "a socially creative and recuperative act"—see Michael Camille and Adrian Rifkin, eds. *Other Objects of Desire: Collectors and Collecting Queerly* (Oxford: Blackwell, 2001).

10 See Sven Spiecker, *The Big Archive: Art From Bureaucracy* (Cambridge, MA: MIT Press, 2008), 56. See also Heather Jackson, *Marginalia: Readers Writing in Books* (Yale

University Press, 2001), for the metaphor, 5–6, 14–15, 26, 81, 84–85, 88, 90–91; and Jacques Derrida, *The Postcard: From Socrates to Freud and Beyond*, trans. Alan Bass (University of Chicago Press, 1987), 210, 216–217.

11 See Benjamin, "Hashish in Marseille," in *Selected Writings*, 677.

12 Cf. Freud's mystic writing pad, "Notes on the Mystic Writing Pad," trans. James Strachey et al., in *The Standard Edition of the Complete Psychological Works of Sigmund Freud*, vol. 19, ed. James Strachey (London: Hogarth Press and Institute of Psycho-Analysis, 1961), 41; see also Spiecker, *The Big Archive*.

13 Pearson and Shanks, *Theatre/Archaeology*, 10; see also Benjamin, "Excavation and Memory" (in *Selected Writings*, 576)—a single page that likens memory to "a man digging," anticipating the connection to archaeology; published in Benjamin's lifetime.

14 *A Midsummer Night's Dream*, Arden 2 edition (Harold F. Brooks, London: Methuen, 1979), 4.2.209–212. Hodgdon, *The Shakespeare Trade* (Philadelphia, PA: University of Pennsylvania Press, 1998), 179–180. For the idea of embodied mind and en-minded body, see Ericka Fischer-Lichte, "Appearing as Embodied Mind: Defining a Weak, a Strong and a Radical Concept of Presence," in Gabriella Giannachi, with Nick Kaye and Michael Shanks (eds.), *Archaeologies of Presence: Art, Performance and the Persistence of Being* (London and New York: Routledge, 2012), 103–118.

15 See Hodgdon, "Thirteen Ways of Looking," 97.

16 Matthew Reason suggests an alternative archive that includes a tableau of remains—objects and costumes—incomplete evidence of what happened. See "Archive or Memory? The Detritus of Live Performance," *New Theatre Quarterly* 19.1 (February 2003), 82–89. See also Carolyn Steedman, *Dust: The Archive and Cultural History* (New Brunswick, NJ: Rutgers University Press, 2002), 154; 68–69.

17 Steedman, *Dust*, 149.

18 *Theatre Journal*, October 1989.

19 For both phrases, see Giannachi et al., *Archaeologies of Presence*, 249.

20 See, for instance, Foucault's discussion of Velasquez's *Las Meninas*: Michel Foucault, *The Order of Things: An Archaeology of the Human Sciences*. [1966] (Paris: Gallimard, 1996), 3–4.

21 See Augusto Boal, *Theatre of the Oppressed*, trans. Charles A. and Maria-Odilia Leal McBride (New York: Theatre Communications Group, 1978 [1973 in Spanish]). See also Rebecca Schneider, *Performance Remains: Art and War in Times of Theatrical Reenactment* (London and New York: Routledge, 2011), and "Performance Remains Again," in *Archaeologies of Presence*, eds. Gabriella Giannachi et al., 64–81.

22 This section is indebted to conversations with Richard Abel.

23 See Benjamin, *The Arcades Project*, trans. Howard Eiland and Kevin McLaughlin (Cambridge, MA: Harvard University Press, 1999), 460 [N1a, B]; and "Unpacking My Library."

24 See Pearson and Shanks, *Theatre/Archaeology*, 43, 58–59. See also Benjamin, *Selected Writings*, 576; and Gay McAuley, *Space in Performance: Making Meaning in the Theatre* (Ann Arbor: University of Michigan Press, 2000).

25 Giannachi et al., *Archaeologies of Presence*, 20.

26 Hodgdon, "Thirteen Ways," 6–7.

27 John Berger, *Another Way of Telling* (New York: Vintage International, 1995), 89.

28 See Frances A. Yates, *The Art of Memory* (Chicago, IL and London: University of Chicago Press, 1966).

29 Hodgdon, "Thirteen Ways," 139.

1

MATERIAL REMAINS AT PLAY[1]

"Our revels now are ended. These our actors . . . / Are melted into air, into thin air; . . . / And like this insubstantial pageant faded, / Leave not a rack behind." The point at which Prospero, anticipating Peggy Phelan by centuries, imagines the disappearance of performance gestures toward the birth of the theatrical archive. Although performance itself may exist merely as memory, dream, mis-recollection, the archives are jam-packed with the shells and shards left behind once actors evacuate the space and time of performance: costumes, properties, set models, sketches and drawings, sound recordings, photographs and documents—everything from rehearsal notes and call sheets to promptbooks and stage managers' reports. Seated in the archive, an open box before me, I am looking at folders filled with tattered, rumple-edged pages not intended for my eyes[2] holding secrets that extend well beyond the familiar pre-planned territory of the backstage tour, its visit to costume and property shops promising an insider's look at theatre-in-the-making. I hear voices: the deputy stage manager who records actors' moves and occasionally talks back (writing "Give us a break, boss" beside Lysander's plea to Theseus in the promptbook for *Midsummer Night's Dream*'s first scene); the dresser detailing personal items and props to be set backstage for Ian McKellen's Romeo ("tissues, Eau-de-cologne, gold spot, honey and spoon, brown packet with sugar in, money, letter, small dagger, large dagger, sword"); the stage manager's report wearily noting that the front-of-house manager's cat (once again) had walked across stage during a *Coriolanus* performance.[3]

Listening to these echoes resembles eavesdropping on one side of a conversation, fragments of performance process, intimations of a theatrical unconscious. These remains—traces endowed with agency—have a staying power in the promptbook as well as in other documents, tracking how written words link to performers' bodies, gestures, behaviors. Rather than using them to reconstruct the performance, my interest lies in mapping the roles such remains play in performance culture.[4]

Taking a cue from Philip Auslander, I view the promptbook neither as giving indexical access to a theatrical past and thus bound up with ontology, nor as archival or documentary, but as a site of re-performance.[5]

In the archive with *Antony and Cleopatra*

On a close summer morning, stillness promising afternoon heat, I am sitting in the Shakespeare Centre Library, the promptbook for Peter Brook's 1978 *Antony and Cleopatra* on the table before me. Weighing a bit over four pounds and showing signs of wear, it is an original: Trevor Williamson, the deputy stage manager (whose name appears on the book's opening pages), constructed it. Used at Stratford's Royal Shakespeare Theatre and also when the production transferred to London's Aldwych Theatre, its pages have been hole-punched and put in a red plastic binder. The New Penguin Shakespeare's front cover has been stuck on the binder's cover; verso pages contain text pages; recto pages contain moves and choreography, written in pen and pencil, with occasional sketches of stage position.[6] When I opened this promptbook, a single unbound sheet, written in a different hand than Williamson's—a post-rehearsal addition?—fell out. It diagrammed positions and noted moves for an initial entry—"As houselights fade, whole company (not Octavia) enter UR and UL led by A + C"—that recalled and repeated the opening of Brook's 1970 *Midsummer Night's Dream*, where (with working lights still up) actors burst through two upstage doors, making the white box suddenly come alive, splashed with a rainbow of arcing colors. If, as Marvin Carlson suggests, live performances are already embodied ghosts, hostage to prior material exigencies, performances and also performance memories,[7] then the material remains surviving performance are ghosts ghosting ghosts—theatre as palimpsest, eternally borrowing, rewriting, re-animating a past performance. As I reached the end of these working papers, I came across the Clown—played by Richard Griffiths, who doubled as the Messenger (another form of ghosting?). Even in this meticulously annotated promptbook, nothing elsewhere offers such a full choreography as Griffiths' extended "asp dance," comprising twenty numbered moves, ending with a fort-da game where looks, gestures and responses for both players receive a descriptive phrase or sentence—"Clown takes lid off basket; Cleopatra takes basket, looks in it, turns it upside down, there is nothing in it. Clown takes R shoe off his hand + produces a snake, puts it in basket; produces last snake from within his costume." Although all the stage manager running the show needs to know is that a pattern of delays, false exits and returns marks and slows the scene, Williamson had an extraordinary sense of the rhythms and timing of this sequence. Why did he so fully document this comic business? Were directorial authority, Williamson's eye for detail or both responsible for recording work that so enhances the performers' authority, saving their invention? Whatever the case, this map of actors' work, a way of telling that captures the orality of rehearsal practice in which words become keys, clues and provocations to action, is so densely detailed that, with a little help from costume, props (basket and snakes), proper shoes and red nose,

I could stand in Griffiths' footprints and re-perform his performance. (By putting myself into his traces, what once belonged to a particular player and performance now belongs (partially) to me: "Me—to play."[8] Archive, then, masquerading as theatre: evoking theatrical metaphors, Jacques Derrida writes, "The question of the archive is not . . . a question of the past. . . . It is a question of the future . . . the question of a response."[9]

Just as a play script remains ripe for repetition—in Richard Schechner's famous claim, "Performance means . . . twice-behaved behavior"[10]—for a potential future staging, the promptbook, its archival avatar, gestures toward a future reenactment. Imagining that possibility sparks a different though also surprisingly similar connection to what I saw from front of house. Now, seeing what makes up that performance and how it is being made, moving backward as well as forward, I am dancing on a different field of play. As I attempt to discern performance's "walking shadows," its subjects and subjectivities, I work toward a performative re-wrighting, re-imagining, replaying, the force of performance processes.

Prompting

Constructed during rehearsals and written in pencil, marked, remarked and over-marked—in the archive I also use a pencil, cross out, begin again, mimicking theatrical practice—the promptbook records rehearsal-room thinking. Even if such information may not appear overtly in performance, as gesture, behavior or speech, it is not only woven into and behind the thickness of what audiences see and hear but also enables retrieving what has been stored. A theatrical analogue to Freud's mystic writing pad, wherein a palimpsestic past is overlaid by present time and timings, it combines essential aspects of memory.[11] This sense of the promptbook as always under reconstruction—fluent, unstable, impermanent, becoming itself through serial disappearances—makes it partially analogous to performance itself. Although more properly called the stage manager's book,[12] since she or he is its end user, there is some advantage to retaining "prompt"—defined as inciting to action, to inspire, giving rise to thought, with connotations of being prompt, ordered and orderly—on time and up to speed. Even better, to my mind is prompt*script*, where "script" signals neither writing nor performance alone . . . neither archive nor repertoire alone, neither object nor performer alone, but moves between and among these ways of thinking through theatre, enacting a kind of joinery.[13] Whereas reading a play allows one to linger, go back, skip ahead, a promptscript's annotations impose a state of being-in-time (and also of being-in-space) onto the writing. Straddling time, existing in interim time, mean-time, exploratory time between rehearsal and live event, the promptscript sutures rehearsal time to performance time, tracks the afterlife of the written words that haunt all Shakespearean performances at the interface of theatrical process. As the promptscript takes on material form, it sculpts time not just through words but also through the various technologies of performance—acting as voice and movement, sound effects, music and light.[14] And just as psychoanalysis has to do with remembering, repeating and working through, so too does the promptscript. Echoing the absent actors, evidence of their bodies is everywhere apparent, marked by trace movements of flesh, muscle, bone, blood and breath. Hot-wired to the actor's performing body, the promptscript rewrites and so controls it,[15] constituting the point of reference for the body's work, which can be measured by as well as against it.

"In good time": *Richard III*

Turning to the promptscript for Richard Eyre's 1990 National Theatre production of *Richard III*, which resituated the play in a "what-if" 1930s Britain under Oswald Mosley's rule[16] and featured Ian McKellen as Richard, I read—again, with a difference—what once happened as re-happening: revival as reenactment or revenant.[17] Just as Carolyn Steedman, reading Derrida, marks the grammatical tense of the archive as the future perfect—"when it will have been"[18]—that sense of time is endemic to *Richard III*, sound-bound to the verse and locked into the play's structure, which moves from Richard's "Why, I, in this weak piping time of peace./Have no delight to pass away the time/Unless to spy my shadow in the sun/And descant on mine own deformity" toward an ending that, exceeding closure, invokes the future, with Richmond's vow to "Enrich the time to come with smooth-faced peace,/With smiling plenty and fair prosperous days." Within that continuum are multiple frames of time—historical time or, in this case, pseudo-historical time, the rhythms of actors' movements in relation to the spatial architecture of the performance space and to other actors, the pulse and force of speech rhythms—all available for remarking at any one moment.[19]

In addition, how spectators sense time and perceive it as a mnemonic engages another sense of time: as Matthew Reason writes, "the performance wasn't really what *was* happening on stage but what *is* happening in the minds and subsequently the memories of the audience."[20] As Peter Handke's *Offending the Audience* insists

> there were always two times: ... the time of the spectators, and the played time, which seemed to be the real time. But time cannot be played. It cannot be repeated in any play. Time is irretrievable. Time is irresistible. Time is unplayable. Time is real. It cannot be played as real.[21]

Looking at the promptscript, however, invites rethinking Handke's conundrum. For not only is the promptscript's subject time itself—time passing not just as a series of distinct, clocked intervals but as an unfolding rhythm according each moment a spatial-temporal depth—but the promptscript's pages record theatrical time as always already occurring in the present tense.

Several senses of time trace through this promptscript's first cues: "On clear from Front of House call [for] ... lights up": "Hear cheering" followed by "Smoke," a quick blackout and "explosion" precede Richard's appearance on an upstage walkway, marking his figure as belonging to and emerging from battle. His costume—khaki breeches and overcoat, Sam Browne belt, leather glove, frog holster with pistol, officer's billed cap—enhances that effect materially long before his first words underscore it. Called "Solo" in the promptscript, which renames each scene with a Brechtian banner—another instance of theatrical rescripting that secures relocation, underscores "about-ness" and suggests motive—the promptscript's markings reveal little or nothing about the form and pressure of what I remember as McKellen's crisp, staccato delivery—almost a monotone. All that appears is that speaking a particular word keys sound and/or light cues; otherwise, the moment belongs to the actor, who shapes the words at will. As Derrida suggests, if one finds nothing but white space, that absence is not *nothing* but rather the space left by what has disappeared: the very emptiness constitutes a sign of how, in performance, the space was once filled and animated.[22]

Speaking shadows

The dresser's notes, however, reveal a precisely articulated shadow performance, a sequence of timed actions making up an invisible spectacle that runs alongside the promptscript.[23] Written on small lined sheets held together with a safety pin, heavily stained, over-written and scripted in minute detail, these notes construct the performer's body as an "object" around which intense attention clusters:

> Ian has to be in his Dressing Room 1 hour before curtain UP. Black elasticated lumbar support (inked in) . . . Ian usually gets dressed at the "quarter" (6:40 p.m.). CHECK, costume, props for costume 1 and remind him to wear pop sock. (Take bayonet with you) (Have white ring and red ring on you).

Another list notes "plastic hump attached to white silky leotard."

At McKellen's exit, his dresser takes his leather glove, gives him the white-stoned gold ring and bayonet and checks props for his second costume:

> 1 white cotton handkerchief (in top pocket of evening tail-coat), small black bible containing Brakenbury note (inside Left Hand pocket of evening tail-coat), 1 white cotton handkerchief (in Right Hand pocket of evening trousers), silver cigarette case containing 3 cigarettes, a silver lighter.

Labeled "Quite quick," the next sequence reads:

> Take cup of water with you to Down Stage Left Assembly, for Quick/ Change into costume 2. Fiona + wigs help you with this change which requires a chair. Ian will exit Down Stage Left and take off Costume 1. F + wigs will concentrate on upper half while you concentrate on removing boots and khaki breeches. Hand him black dress Trousers, boots + red-stoned gold ring. Jacket; check back/front of shirt for fit [Do up bow tie at back] marginal note: Don't set change on seat of chair as he sits down.

Just as reading dresser's notes detail invisible labor and make hidden time-sequences visible, bringing both into theatrical consciousness, the promptscript also highlights more obvious timing patterns—rhythms of setting and striking furniture and props, bringing objects on and carrying them off—action sequences in space performed, in this case, by actors as well as stagehands—here, five men in black.

But what seems especially intriguing is how, from the outset, the rhythms of Richard's speech and actions determine, even command, the entire performance: his entrances and exits script even the movements of dressers and stage crew who put costumes and properties in place. Time, here, is Richard's time—at least until Tudor history appears on the horizon to overwhelm him, at which point rhythmic control, especially as indicated by light and sound cues, swings between Richard and Richmond. Aside from the scene of the mourning queens, called "Greenham Common"—evoking a time and place where the Women's Peace Camp gathered to protest nuclear weapons being placed at an RAF base (1982)—those scenes featuring Richard—"Solo," "Mortuary," "Dinner Party," "Family Photo," "Victoria Station," "Strawberries," "Under the Table," "Up to the Leads," "Coronation," "Camps and Dreams," "Battles"—total over two hours of the 190-minute running time noted in stage manager's reports, leaving only a spare hour for others to bustle in.[24]

Is there a pattern here, built into the playscript's structure? If so, heavy cuts also have shaped that script to heighten Richard's monomania, further enhanced by the production's emphasis on physicality and its often highly technical look. As Thomas Heywood reports, the player "commands our attention: sit in a full theatre, and you will think you see so many lines drawn from the circumference of so many ears, while the actor is the center."[25] Now as then, promptscript and performance are "about" spending time with Richard; strictly regimented throughout, this conception of time is "something 'created' via body and brain"[26] and ties into a spectator's perception—that is, Richard *takes up* a certain amount of time. Not only does he run the show, he also constitutes its chief special effect, in control of and controlled by light and sound plots, which intensify the mode or aura of his body, change its tension—and tense.

An instance occurs at the Dinner Party when, with King Edward nearing death, the others exit, leaving Richard alone. "I do the wrong, and first begin to broil," he begins, crossing to each of four three-branched candelabra in turn and blowing each candle out—the next-to-last group as he names "Rivers . . . Dorset . . . Grey"—before smothering the last three ("And seem a saint, when most I play the devil") with a napkin. Required by law, a document entitled "Use of Naked Flame" maps the start-to-finish timing:

> 1 single candelabra carried on from Down Stage Right by Susan Engel (Queen Margaret), puts down on Stage Right end of table where it remains approximately 16 min. during the action of the scene, the candles are extinguished by . . . Ian McKellen 15 minutes, 15½ minutes 15¼ minutes and 16 minutes later.

When Richard snuffs out the flames, he is performing murder but nonetheless acting in accordance with the regulations and procedures designed to protect actors' bodies from the dangerous proximity of fire. The use of flame here echoes in "Greenham Common," where the Duchess of York, Queen Margaret and Queen Elizabeth kneel before trays on which the number of lighted candles for each represents their dead husbands and children. Just as Stanislavski breaks down text into rhythmic micro-units of physical action,[27] the interplay of light mimics that strategy within the architecture of the performance space.[28] The general formula for the "Dinner Party's" tightly orchestrated choreography—"wait for Richard to speak and do X, then GO"—is premised, as is any cue, entirely on what the performer says and does—and, coincidentally, on the possibility of his (or her) failure to do so. This light will fall *here* when and if and *only* if he speaks, moves or gestures—just *there*—to make the effect happen. And as this scene concludes, McKellen's trajectory from left to right stage, moving against the spectator's usual way of reading the stage, enhances the intense deliberation—and perversity—of his plotting.

A similar intensity bleeds into John Haynes' photograph of McKellen. Reading it through a convergence of document and image as the prompscript's supplement or inter(in)animated mnemonic, I move across time.[29] In memory, time often

FIGURE 1.1   Ian McKellen as Richard III in the "dinner scene" from *Richard III*, directed by Richard Eyre (National Theatre 1990). Photo: © John Haynes and the National Theatre.

stands still, which perhaps is why the theatre photograph, in which time collapses, solidifies and gets compressed, circulates in the marketplace, where, as synecdoche for the live encounter, it sells performance by grabbing its temporal fragments. Looking generates an immediacy, what Walter Benjamin calls the "still real"—that is, the future subsists not just *in* the photograph but *through* the viewer who discovers it as still, in the sense of *still remaining*, thus suspending the onlooker between performance history and the immediate *now*.[30] Interrogating economies of time, revealing agency, it bears witness to actions noted in the promptscript, reveals how lighting drives vision.[31] As light is brought to prominent attention, the image reads as though the specter of Othello—"put out the light ... and then ... put out the light"—and that of McKellen's Iago had suddenly played unscripted roles.[32] In this potentially obscene though mesmerizing gesture, is light punctuating space and speech or is it the other way around? Captured in intense immobility, McKellen's Richard cannot move to the next frame but remains freeze-framed in time, candlelight sculpting the motionless, made-up face into a mask, McKellen as the specter of Richard, the trace of red on his dress shirt an accidental prolepsis of his death.

In contrast to this precise choreography, the promptscript for Richard's "wooing" of Lady Anne remains surprisingly silent as to recording theatrical technologies—two light cues frame their encounter—or of figuring a word or line. Only two pauses occur: one before Anne's "Would they were basilisks, to strike thee dead"; the other before Richard's "Vouchsafe to wear this ring"—elongated instances of affective silence. Strikingly, Anne's pause notes the *single* trace of her promptscript presence—a sign of the performer's freedom and, beyond that, proleptically anticipating her death at Richard's hands. Any further annotations map Richard's moves, his use of costume and hand properties:

> Wipe eyes with hanky; Moving closer to her; Takes off Jacket, hands Anne sword; Kneels and faces her; Removes ring and hands it out to Lady Anne then puts it on her finger; £5 note to stretcher bearers at their exit; Richard cross to Down Centre, puts jacket etc back on.

Yet even this account of behavior gestures toward absence, glosses an act of kinesthetic imagining[33] in which everyday habits of unbuttoning, buttoning up and reordering clothing expand textual and theatrical space and time, generating what becomes a powerful mnemonic trace of live performance.

A trace of that trace, as costume and body parts, appears in Neil Libbert's rehearsal photograph of Eve Matheson and McKellen—a shot which serves as both stand-in and supplement for the promptscript's empty spaces. An image par excellence of looking at performance in reverse, a rehearsal photograph generates the illusion of giving entrée into the mysteries of the performer's craft at a moment when no one, supposedly, is looking. Unfinished, brought before its time into view, it captures the performers in the act of thinking through attitude, pose and gesture. Is there a kinesthesia of thought? I think there is—one that registers, in part, the

FIGURE 1.2 Ian McKellen (Richard III) and Eve Matheson (Lady Anne) in rehearsal
for *Richard III*, directed by Richard Eyre (National Theatre 1990). Photo:
© Neil Libbert and the National Theatre.

difference between sketch and finished painting. Like a promptscript, this still is a
"scriptive thing,"[34] a fleshy document inscribing the complicity of this encounter
at the prescient moment when both performers are in the process of annexing
Richard and Anne to themselves, discovering how their bodies occupy space—
come together, stay apart—who initiates movement, who follows, who is passive,
who active, who is to be looked at, who is doing the looking.[35] Not only is the
space between the two tautly charged as though invisible threads join them but this
is a mirror image that is not quite a mirror image, in which the performers' clasped
hands complement—and contradict—each other. McKellen is in the dominant,
right-frame position, but although he looks straight at Matheson, his lowered head
makes him the object of her (hidden) gaze—the looked-on not the looker—and of
her silent, unspoken voice. If, as in Peggy Phelan's paraphrase of Baudrillard's claim
that "seduction is the realm of the reversible . . . ruled by the feminine, manipulat[ing]
appearances by mastering them,"[36] does McKellen's gesture, covering his sex with
his hands, suggest that he is playing the woman, pretending perfect abjection?

Yet what I find most arresting about this image—what Roland Barthes calls a
punctum, or wound, the detail that suddenly, paradoxically expands to fill the whole
frame, becoming the thing itself—are Matheson's hands, clasped behind her back.[37]
Is she already bound or does she keep herself tightly reined in so that she does not
strike out? The one gesture appears latent in the other, lending her agency, which
not only illuminates the sense of the scene but, as memory flashes up in a
moment of danger,"[38] becomes the residue through which memory sutures to
performance time. In the lightning-like power of that expansion, my vision
becomes Bottom-like: I *re-hear* the scene and *re-see* its spoken words as the actors
build to a key image, holding it in tension before allowing it to dissolve.[39] Yet what

I am experiencing is not live performance but its cinematic avatar, Richard Loncraine's 1996 film,[40] in which McKellen gives the scene to Kristen Scott-Thomas, its moves reminiscent of Hepburn–Tracy comedies and Grant–Russell chases around tables or desks[41] until, as Richard speaks of his face wet with tears at his father's death ("like trees bedashed with rain"), he evokes Anne's sympathy.

Just as the rehearsal photography gives (stilled) life to how theatrical process marries performance time, the promptscript, dresser's notes and fight-script annotate Richard's death, each somewhat differently. As though recalling Michael Bogdanov's *Richard III*,[42] killing the king disrupts established temporal relationships, jolts rapidly backward from the 1930s to the medieval "full-metal-jacket" killing time of an epic 1485 Bosworth Field. With McKellen already dressed in a custom-made Gothic suit of armor[43] and just prior to the fight's final stages, an equally rapid costume change marks that time-shift:

> Ian exits Up Stage Right. Wigs take off wig. You put on black skullcap and bow tie it under chin. Wigs drape bloodied scarf around his neck. Help Ian with helmet. This needs to be pushed firmly down—press hard on his head—and fastened with Velcro strap under his chin. Jane hands him bloodied sword.

At this point, the promptscript mimics the text's "*They fight*," followed by a spare summary: "Stanley spears Richard then all Richmond soldiers rush in on Richard + stab him: break away. Stanley last person to pull spear out." The finish? A cartoon-like "death tableau" of a stick figure, head toward the audience, a tiny dagger beside him, offhandedly captioned, "Richard dies DA DA DA DA!"

Whereas Richard's time and timing have, throughout, seemed to expand performance time, it now contracts. John Waller's fight choreography maps the inner dynamic of battle through a tightly edited sequence of short combats woven together, the rapid change from one move to another generating a time-scape of Bosworth's legendary battle that meticulously measures out Richard's death through a series of coded gestures that are precisely subject to three and a half minutes of time. Like performance, the fight is an event that enacts its disappearance in the very act of its materializing. Intimately attuned to the speed of the body, the speed of foot and hand, the fight script is a hyper-instance of bodily inscription, requiring participants to pay heightened attention to body memory. Looking at how the document disarticulates the event into individual moves lays bare a sequential sense of the moving body put into slow-motion replay, returns one to a sense of theatrical processes that, once hidden, were impossible to absorb visually when they occurred. Altogether comprising some 115 separate moves, excluding the rushes when Richmond's forces move in on Richard en masse, the overall rhythm of this final dance mimics individual thrusts of sword and spear. It happens very fast: two to three moves per second within 210 seconds of playing time. And Waller's script gives only actors' names and/or initials—a notational trace of the real behind the role, the tenuous splice, doubling up signifier and signified, upon which theatre depends. And at the very last, "COLIN [Richmond] (without helm) pulls them off and kneeling over or beside Ian, smashes Ian's head on floor. (Eye contact—Ian does it)." Although it's a theatrical trick, McKellen's "doing" confirms that this Richard's death comes on his own terms, in his own time and timing.

As performance travels away from itself toward a seizure of the real, it is not the promptscript but dresser's notes that choreograph the curtain call, tracking the passage of "Richard" to his vanishing point: "Ian will exit Down Stage Right. You will need a chair for him to sit on [underlining in original]. Help him off with helmet and black skullcap. Wigs will replace wig while you undo his left arm armour fitting. Remind him to take off gauntlet." Just as the curtain call is "a seam in social nature ... a beginning and an ending, a return and farewell,"[44] it also represents a place of and for joining where the seam between character and performer opens up: "Ian will exit Down Stage Right. Help him off with remainder of armour. Return with him to Dressing Room and get him out of costume." And as the hand labor of disassembling character through undressing and unmasking devolves into the after-effects of separation, mundane details of fixing and reweaving, preparatory to beginning again: "Collect all washing and hang up all costumes. Return any to wardrobe for drying or repair." "Best of British!!!" reads a possibly ironic tag-line,[45] capped, in another set of notes, by a reminder to ask for tea and coffee money—12p for tea, 15p for coffee—a pittance even smaller than an early modern joiner's four pence a day and food.

Archival play

In closing, I want to move from looking at privileged archival remains to a document surviving from *Richard III, His Death*, in Adrian Noble's trilogy, *The Plantagenets* (RSC 1989)—the record of Ian Barber, a handcraft man who assisted performance process, a rehearsal-room joker who is both inside and outside the theatrical frame:

> Then, at the end, after that nasty big bad mean Richmond kills nice sweet Richard the tent flies out to reveal Ghosts big FX, lots for me to Q. Richmond does last speech. Yawn. Yawn. Rapturouse [*sic*] applause—standing ovation calls of "D.S.M., D.S.M." Me brought on stage showered with flowers, champagne and praise. Signal to rest of staff in wings—I'm lifted high + carried off to "Sardis"—more champagne + praise then home to bed. And it's all done in the best possible taste.[46]

Putting on a discursive mask, this joiner-promptscript-maker constructs a self-seducing fantasy that imagines fulfilling his desire to replace, equal or be the star. And through a serendipitous quirk of archival logic, he signs his real name: "Ian." Inscribing himself into a celebrity moment, he conjures another curtain call that extends and exceeds the performance, even relocates it to another continent. As in striptease, the performance ends not with seeing and knowing all, but with desire. Does that desire, I wonder, resemble mine?

As I write, Bottom the Weaver slips into view. Striving to make sense of his dream—"Methought I was—and methought I had . . ."—he lights on the idea of asking Peter Quince to write a ballad of his "most rare vision" that will embody his experience, translate its seemingly surreal fragments to a form that will generate another performance—a performance about a performance. At a grand and glorious occasion taking place in some future time, Bottom imagines having a great triumph as he sings the ballad "in the latter end of a play before the Duke." For Bottom, as for his surrogate Ian, re-performative writing results in another historically located material practice. As for me, to play again in the archive entails creating networks of configuration that release documents from the house arrest Derrida sees as their intractable condition to give performance remains a present presence. In such work lies another way of telling, and writing, a deeply material performance history.

Notes

1 This chapter reworks an essay first published in *Theatre Journal* 64.3 (October 2012), 373–388.
2 Carolyn Steedman, *Dust: The Archive and Cultural History* (New Brunswick, NJ: Rutgers University Press, 2002), 149.
3 Promptbook for Peter Brook's *Dream* (RSC 1970); dresser's notes for McKellen's *Romeo* (RSC 1976); stage manager's report for *Coriolanus* (RSC 1977).
4 Because *theatre* and *performance* take on particular leverage in performance studies, connoting, on the one hand, pre-scripted events and, on the other, unscripted events—the realm of the explicit, often autobiographical body working without a textual net—I use "performance" as a borderland term that, Janus-like, faces both ways.
5 Auslander writes: "It may well be that our sense of the presence, power, and authenticity of [performance pieces] derives not from treating the document as an indexical access point to a past event but from perceiving the document itself *as a performance* that directly reflects an artist's aesthetic project or sensibility and for which we are the present audience"—see "The Performativity of Performance Documentation," *Performing Arts Journal (PAJ)* 84.3 (2006), 9; emphasis in original. Unlike Auslander, I do not view these documents as direct reflections of an artist's aesthetic project or sensibility.
6 A separate stage manager's script for 1978, also an original, has text on recto pages; verso pages list choreography, cues and props.
7 Marvin Carlson, *The Haunted Stage: The Theatre as Memory Machine* (Ann Arbor, MI: University of Michigan Press, 2003).
8 Hamm's first words in Samuel Beckett's *Endgame* (New York: Grove Press, 1968), 2.
9 Derrida, *Archive Fever: A Freudian Impression*, trans. Eric Presnowitz (Chicago, IL: University of Chicago Press, 1998), 36.
10 Schechner, *Between Theatre and Anthropology* (Philadelphia, PA: University of Pennsylvania Press, 1985), 36–37.
11 Sigmund Freud, "Notes on the Mystic Writing-Pad," trans. James Strachey et al., in *The Standard Edition of the Complete Psychological Works of Sigmund Freud*, vol. 19, ed. James Strachey (London: Hogarth Press and Institute of Psycho-Analysis, 1961), 225–232. I also am indebted to W.B. Worthen and to several of his essays: "Shakespeare/Performance Studies" in *The Shakespeare International Yearbook*, vol. 10 (Burlington, VT: Ashgate, 2009), 77–92, and "Antigone's Bones," *The Drama Review (TDR)* 52.3 (2008), 10–33.
12 Even more properly, the promptbook is the director's property. Terry Hands recalls that, at the RSC during the 1970s and 1980s, directorial contracts carried a clause stating that the director receive a copy of the promptbook, a stipulation that renders the promptbook

intellectual property and effects a loose form of copyright. At the National Theatre Archive, permission to reproduce promptbook pages comes from a production's director.

13 I borrow Robin Bernstein's explanation for using "script," combined with my paraphrase. See her "Dances with Things: Material Culture and the Performance of Race," *Social Text* 27.4 (2009), 94, n69.

14 See Andrei Tarkovsky, *Sculpting in Time: Reflections on the Cinema*, trans. Kitty Hunter-Blair (London: Bodley Head, 1986).

15 I do not mean to suggest a rigid equation between prompt and performance; leeway occurs when actors expand business or hurry through vocal delivery—which accounts for slight variations in running times. Differences also pertain between what is written down and what an archival video reveals about *one* particular performance, depending upon when, during the course of a run, it was filmed. In addition, changes that might occur during previews may or may not be recorded. So although one can assert that the promptscript is a document bound up with rehearsal, it bears a somewhat slippery relation to performance.

16 Mosley formed the British Union of Fascists in 1932; his 1936 challenge to East London resulted in the rout of the Blackshirts. See, for instance, *The Daily Worker*, October 5, 1936.

17 This prompscript is not taken from a published edition but instead follows what has become, within the last fifteen years, a standard practice: a typescript that represents an eclectic text, already incorporating director's cuts or additions. Moreover, it is not an original used to cue performance: although an original sometimes finds its way to the archive, by the end of the run, the working copy of the typescript usually is in such poor condition that it is either discarded or, say, kept by a member of the production team. What readers see, however, is a pristine replica of the original, with every annotation copied out exactly, transcribed by the production department following the performance run; it is in a ring binder, with markings in pen and pencil. My thanks to Elena Carter, archive assistant at the National Theatre Archive, for this information.

18 Steedman, *Dust*, 7.

19 See Bruce R. Smith, "Ragging *Twelfth Night* 1602, 1996, 2002–03," in *A Companion to Shakespeare and Performance*, ed. Barbara Hodgdon and W.B. Worthen (Oxford: Blackwell Publishing, 2005), esp. 59–60.

20 Reason, "Archive or Memory? The Detritus of Live Performance," *New Theatre Quarterly* 19.1 (2003), 86, emphasis in original. See also Eugenio Barba, "Four Spectators," *TDR* 34.1 (1990), 96–101.

21 Handke, *Offending the Audience*, in *Plays I* (London: Methuen, 1997), 24.

22 I borrow Steedman's paraphrase of Derrida: *Dust*, 11.

23 Dresser's notes occur infrequently in archival holdings; those for this Richard III were bundled with the promptscript and other documents related to a world tour and are presumably intended to instruct dressers other than the original crew at each new venue. Only rarely does a dresser's name appear in theatrical records; when she is remembered, as in an autograph book kept by Marian Vale-Humphreys, an RSC dresser from 1923–1972, the names of those who signed her book, from Balliol Holloway to Peggy Ashcroft— "with love from her Shrew"—occlude her own, give her name meaning.

24 Gesturing toward offstage time and sometimes depending on venue, such precise attention to timing may even anticipate or be mindful of transport schedules.

25 *Apology for Actors* (1612), rpt. (London: Shakespeare Society, 1841), 88.

26 See George Lakoff and Mark Johnson, *Philosophy in the Flesh: The Embodied Mind and Its Challenge to Western Thought* (New York: Basic Books, 1999), 169. The actor's body is inherently double, in that it is not a natural body; rather, the actor turns the movements of his body into a metaphor for his role.

27 Stanislavski defines this as "tempo-rhythm": "Stage action, like speech, must be musical. Movement must follow a continuous line, like a note from a stringed instrument, or, when necessary, stop short like the staccato of a coloratura soprano. . . . Movements have their legato, staccato, andante, allegro, piano and forte and so on." See *Sobrani Sochinenii*,

9 vols. (Moscow: Isskustvo, 1951–1964), 1: 387, quoted in Jean Benedetti, *Stanislavski: An Introduction* (London and New York: Routledge, 2004), 69.

28 Jean Kalman designed the production's lighting.

29 I borrow "inter(in)animated" from Rebecca Schneider, *Performance Remains: Art and War in Times of Theatrical Reenactment* (London and New York: Routledge, 2011), 7, 108.

30 Benjamin, "Little History of Photography," in *Selected Writings* vol. 2, Part 2, 1931–1934, trans. Rodney Livingston and Others, eds. Michael W. Jennings, Howard Eiland, and Gary Smith (Cambridge, MA and London: The Belknap Press of Harvard University Press, 1999), 507–530. Benjamin calls this phenomenon "a dialectical image . . . wherein what has been comes together in a flash with the now to form a constellation." See *The Arcades Project*, trans. Howard Eiland and Kevin McLaughlin (Cambridge, MA: Harvard University Press, 1999), 462.

31 See Maurice Merleau-Ponty, *Phenomenology of Perception*, trans. Colin Smith (New York: Humanities Press, 1970), 234–235, 310; cited in Bert O. States, *Great Reckonings in Little Rooms: On the Phenomenology of Theater* (Berkeley, CA: University of California Press, 1985), 51.

32 McKellen played Iago in Trevor Nunn's *Othello* (RSC, 1989).

33 For brilliant readings of kinesthesia, see Susan Leigh Foster, *Choreographing Empathy: Kinesthesia in Performance* (London and New York: Routledge, 2011).

34 I borrow "scriptive thing" from Bernstein, "Dances with Things," 69; and "fleshy document" from Schneider, *Performance Remains*, 37.

35 Susan Leigh Foster, "Choreographies of Gender," *Signs: Journal of Women in Culture and Society* 24.1 (1998), 6–8.

36 Jean Baudrillard, *Seduction*, trans. Brian Singer (New York: St. Martin's Press, 1996; originally published in 1990), paraphrased in Peggy Phelan, *Unmarked: The Politics of Performance* (London and New York, 1993), 123.

37 Barthes, *Camera Lucida: Reflections on Photography*, trans. Richard Howard (New York: Hill and Wang, 1981), 26, 45. Casting Matheson, at this time not a well-known actor, signals the status of Anne's role in relation to McKellen's Richard.

38 I borrow the phrase from Walter Benjamin's "Theses on the Philosophy of History, VI," in *Illuminations*, trans. Harry Zohn, 1955 rpt. (New York: Schocken Books, 1969), 255.

39 See States, *Great Reckonings*, 51–52.

40 An archival video of Eyre's production, the first made for the V&A Theatre and Performance Archive, does exist, but the single camera position, fuzzy image and poor sound quality mar its use-value.

41 In particular, Howard Hawks' *His Girl Friday* (1940).

42 For the English Shakespeare Company's (ESC) *Wars of the Roses*, in which the scene moved from contemporary business suits and desk-top computers to a medieval Bosworth and then back to a working TV studio for the production's final moments.

43 Other armor included a custom-plate steel suit of armor for Richmond, eight back/front breastplates, eight Barbuta helmets (lighter finish with center seam) and ten Salet helmets with visors.

44 States, *Great Reckonings*, 198.

45 Usually, the phrase connotes (ironically) "Good luck"; it also is used un-ironically, for marketing food: "Buy the Best of British." My thanks to Peter Holland for "translating" the idiom.

46 The final line belongs to Kenny Everett's character, Cupid Stunt.

2

REHEARSAL REMAINS OR READING FROM THE MARGINS

Actors' scripts

Although mainstream performance history tends to treat rehearsal as a way station to performance, with the relation between the two emerging as the proper subject of inquiry, I regard rehearsal and consequently its scripts as having value and integrity as sites of presence in themselves—especially resonant in the case of Shakespeare's plays, where roles and performances already reveal traces of past and future iterations. Such documents address an imagined, anticipated rehearsal room audience, performing in the now before those insider witnesses (players, directors, deputy stage managers, stage managers) who will eventually join other spectators in three to six weeks' time (or more) in the more expansive space of stage performance. When brought into the now, what does a player's presence *do* to a Shakespearean text? The majority of Shakespearean performances, after all, begin with a player reading and annotating a script, engaging in "a responsive kind of writing anchored to pre-existing words."[1] Those annotations are fixed to a particular time of writing— "words carry their present [and, I would add, presence] with them," writes Arlette Farge[2]—markers which not only trace bodies but also impose a state of being-in-time and also of being-in-space, onto the writing. Even in the sparest annotated script, two voices always are operating: the annotator talking to herself or himself—and/ or to the author or adaptor. Engaging with those traces, I join the conversation, talking back to another's reading and to Shakespeare. To take this idea further is to say that the script is a paper stage and to imagine the archive as a theatre of encounter[3] which brings a fleeting assemblage of voices into visibility, unsettling expectations of singular meanings.

Memory and history

I begin with Ellen Terry's 1906 script for Hermione in *Winter's Tale*, which exists as twelve "rolls" reminiscent of early modern theatrical texts—not only because it

FIGURE 2.1   Edward Alleyn, cropped from a Token Book at the London Metropolitan
Archives, City of London, Parish records of Saint Saviour Southwark.
Reproduced by kind permission of the Chapter of Southwark Cathedral.

is a cue script, which gives the last two or three words of the previous speaker's
part as a prompt for the next speaker's delivery, but also because it brings into view
the only actor's part that has survived from the sixteenth or early seventeenth
century—*Orlando Furioso*, with annotations thought to be in Edward Alleyn's
hand[4]—a proto-cue script that also proleptically looks forward to other codes
for marking a script: positional markings and scribbled annotations typical of a
present-day performer's rehearsal script as well as two theatrical mnemonics,
underlining and copying out, which still remain in use today. Both are means of
taking possession—versions of signing one's name in a new book—so announcing
the player's presence. In Farge's elegantly succinct phrase, copying out is "an exclu-
sive and privileged way of entering into the world of the document, as both
accomplice and outsider."[5]

Physically copying a passage permits me to become directly involved, to
integrate textuality within my performative fantasy, even to positioning myself
"within" the text: this is not just a means of identification or empathy with an
event or character but a form of self-enactment comparable to an Austinian
speech-act: straddling the literary and the theatrical, language performs.[6] Writing
to John Taylor, John Philip Kemble cites a pure instance of this phenomenon, a
theatrical madeleine of sorts: "I have copied the part of Hamlet forty times, and
you have obliged me to consider and copy it once more."[7] John Gielgud copies
out his lines—in a beautifully elegant hand, retaining its verse or prose form and

its punctuation—on the verso pages of his surviving scripts. Since I have as yet been unable to find a *Shakespeare* script with Gielgud's copying-out or annotations, it is tempting to conjecture that Shakespearean tones and intonations have become so deeply engraved in his cognitive pathways that he has no need of a written mnemonic. As for underlining, in most present-day scripts I have seen, the player has underlined her/his part. Notably, Gielgud's script for *Bingo*,[8] which comes as close as possible to marking his Shakespeare connection, carries markings for minimal moves but few other annotations. What it does reveal, though the practice is hardly consistent throughout, is that he has copied out his speeches on the verso page, underlining verbs and, often, those nouns or phrases that close a sentence and/or call attention to its meaning, as in "I'm protecting my own interests. Not supporting you, or fighting the town" (1.1.7). If Gielgud did annotate a Shakespeare text, I would conjecture that it might well contain minimal indications of pause and stress—that he may well have internalized both. That scripts survive at all seems purely accidental: handed over as part of paper legacies left as endowments, some turn up in official archives—the British Library, the V&A's Theatre and Performance Archive—or are boxed or squirreled away in private archives. Here, underlining and copying-out connect to and assume the speed of the body: linked to the personal, handwriting is to space what the voice is to time.[9]

Parting Hermione (1906)

Somewhat remarkably, 300 years later, Ellen Terry's cue-script for Hermione (1906) represents a direct descendent of the 1592 "Orlando" part, which represented a formula that apparently saw little change over time. Inscribed on extremely thin 10 × 5¼ pages, Terry's thick black writing (in ink?) marches across the long side of each of twelve pages, averaging a dozen lines per page; cues are heralded by a long preceding heavy line (the "tail") moving from left to right, directing attention to the cue word or phrase, aligned at right.[10] On pages eleven and twelve, the writing, though clearly in the same hand, is distinctly lighter. Minimal annotations occur throughout: most frequent are those marking emphases with double or triple underlining; exit cues also are set apart, framed in heavily outlined square brackets. At "One of them you shall be (**witty—sprightly**)" (1.2.56), the parenthetical reminder of vocal tone appears in heavy black ink, as does "**LORDINGS**," re-printed at the end of "You were pretty lordings then?" (1.2.62),[11] possibly to clarify the handwriting.

Hermione's part (comparable to 1.2, 2.1 and 3.2) comprises the scenes containing *most* of her role, save for what she speaks when she returns to life at the play's close. I say most of her role because Herbert Beerbohm Tree's severe cutting tailors Hermione as an impeccably chaste wife, incapable of voicing risqué thoughts, and removes any suggestion, even in playful teasing, that she has committed adultery.[12] The cuts carry a chain of allusions that begin as Hermione asks Polixenes if he and Leontes have "tripped" (that is, had sex) since their innocent boyhood. Her wordplay continues, piling up further allusions—to devils, temptresses, offences, sins, faults—their sense dependent on whether Leontes hears and what he believes.[13] Moreover, the last page of the cue-script stops short part way through Hermione's response to Leontes' accusations and unlawful treatment.[14] And at the news of Mamillius' death (3.2.144), she faints, so that her role appears to end with verbal silence, a "death" twinned with that of her son.[15] Since Tree cut half the text in order to accommodate spectacular sets, that cut-off point may or may not be accidental. And what if one adopted an interactive reading practice? Might Terry have convinced Tree to reinstate lines struck from the part? She writes of playing Beatrice to Henry Irving's Benedick and refusing to perform a gag she thought demeaning to the character, but when Irving insisted that she play the gag, she reluctantly succumbed.[16] Yet by 1906, given her phenomenal success as Portia, both in Squire Bancroft's adaptation (1875) at the Prince of Wales's Theatre and at the Lyceum with Irving (1879), which ran for a record number of performances,[17] would Terry have accrued enough theatrical capital to argue for restoring lines she saw as crucial to her view of the character—to "doing it her way"? Yet in either case, Tree's version of Hermione's part derives from a masculinist reading of her role—or, more specifically, Hermione as seen exclusively through Leontes' eyes. Given this minimalist document, outside evidence fleshes out Hermione's part in the cue script. Madeleine Bingham, for instance, quotes a *Daily Telegraph* review of her presence: "She came before us a woman clothed in white samite, mystic wonderful—pleading with proud dignity for her innocence and the blamelessness of her life." Was this also, perhaps, the moment Christopher St. John remembered, writing that Terry's Hermione reminded him of a statue of Niobe in the Louvre?[18]

Picture-perfect Portia

Terry's script for Portia is on 10¾ × 6¼ printed pages with the fragility of onion-skin paper; each is headed *Merchant of Venice*, centered on the page, numbered 33–58 in the upper right corner and tied together at three points with twine.[19] Beginning *in medias res* with Bassanio's casket-choosing (3.2 in a modern text), it ends in disarray following twenty lines of 5.1, Jessica and Lorenzo talking of famous lovers, and is shot through with cuts and doubles, so that reading is characterized by the advances and retreats associated with processes of poaching.[20] Although it is difficult to be certain about the provenance of this incomplete document, an informed guess suggests that the script represents a pared-down "cut-and-paste" version of Charles Kean's 1858 *Merchant*, staged at the Princess's Theatre.[21] Although it may not properly be called a rehearsal script, that term conveniently points to its probable use. Yet, since sections mentioned in various accounts are missing—Portia's dialogue with Nerissa about the unsuitable suitors (1.2)[22] and the finale in Belmont's garden, for instance—the script is perhaps best characterized as partial remains. Most annotations resemble known examples of Terry's hand.[23] Some, however, have been made with different writing instruments, perhaps written in a different hand and at different times, creating a deeply layered text. After all, a rehearsal script is always under re-construction—fluent, unstable, becoming itself through serial disappearances—making it analogous to performance itself. Except where noted otherwise, moves follow the entries and exits as printed; act and scene notations appear in bold at the top of each page and the pages, but not the lines, are numbered.

The joy of reading

Reading Portia's part, then, entails wandering through several layers of annotation, some of which are not exclusively tied to her role but pertain to those of other players—reader as *flaneuse*. Something of a curiosity, Terry's *Merchant* script does not align either with the printed playtext—changes occur in stage directions; several scenes are crossed out—or with descriptions of performance—for instance, a note about "casket music" associated with Morocco's choice suggests that he was present, but the script includes only one of his lines.[24] Perhaps most curiously "there but not there" are Jessica and Lorenzo: although both roles appear on the printed pages, they are selectively crossed out or over-written: Jessica appears to drop out entirely and "Solanio" is written in over Lorenzo's name. This brief preface to Squire Bancroft's rearrangement and adaptation of *Merchant*, a version that reduced twenty scenes to seven (perhaps to avoid scene changes in view of the audience),[25] aimed for the utmost realism. Relying heavily on Edward Godwin's expert advice, Bancroft commissioned George Gordon and William Harford to send assistants to Venice to sketch archaeologically authentic locales, which then appeared on painted drop curtains as a means of moving from one scene to another.[26] Terry wrote: "A more gorgeous and complete little spectacle had never been seen on the English stage. Veronese's *Marriage at Cana* had inspired many of the stage pictures, and the expenditures in carrying them out had been lavish."[27] Wrote Bancroft:

> It all looked so unlike a theatre, and so much more like old Italian pictures than anything that had been previously shown on the stage.... It may be that it all came a little before the proper time, and that we saw things too far in advance.[28]

Bancroft's post-performance justification aside, the idea that *Merchant* was ahead of its time is not wholly far-fetched: contemporary audiences were flocking to dioramas, and it would not be long before those stilled pictures would move—if not speak.

Bancroft claimed that he had not altered a single syllable of Shakespeare's text and that only transpositions of the dialogue figured in his re-arrangement of the play.[29] There is, of course, an obvious contradiction between such claims and knowing that Charles Kean's 1858 *Merchant* lies obscured beneath them. "Perhaps," he remarked, "there will be no better opportunity to describe the sequence of scenes I eventually decided on, for I often have regretted that I did not print the play as we produced it"[30]—a statement that raises questions about the script's status. The most striking transpositions occurred in the casket choosing: material for an editor's nightmare. Beginning with Morocco's "Who chooseth me will gain what many men desire," the text continues with Arragon's "That 'many' may be meant/ By the fool multitude that choose by show" and then to a composite passage comprising the terms of the choice—"I am enjoined by oath to observe three things . . . fortune now/To my heart's hope!—gold, silver, and base lead," which then incorporates Portia's reminder of his oath.[31] Bancroft re-assigns all these lines to Bassanio, but the entire passage is crossed out, so that the casket choosing opens with Portia's "I pray you, tarry; pause a day or two." Proceeding by fugitive fits and starts, this bricolage stands as a prime example of the poaching processes endemic to this *Merchant* script.

The look of the play and the player

Additional information, drawn primarily from Bancroft's post-performance commentaries and Godwin's descriptions of architecture and costume, not only fleshes out a partial narrative arc but also resembles raiding more accurately than poaching. What initially stands out are descriptions of what Terry looked like and what she wore. "As the curtain rose upon Nell's tall and slender figure in a china-blue and white brocade gown, a red rose at her breast, the whole house burst forth in rapturous applause."[32] Terry herself glossed her roles in terms of clothes. When Terry played Titania at Bath's Theatre Royal (1863), she wrote: "This was the first lovely dress I ever wore and I learned a great deal from it."[33] Elsewhere, she remarks, "In the casket scene I wore a dress like almond-blossom . . . [and] moved and spoke slowly. The clothes seemed to demand it, and the setting of the play developed the Italian feeling in it, and let the English Elizabethan element take care of itself." For Terry, Portia is "the child of a period of beautiful clothes, beautiful cities, beautiful houses, beautiful ideas. She speaks the beautiful language of inspired poetry."[34] Dressing up for the part, she became part of the scenery: to-be-looked-at, a spectacle.[35] A review bears this out:

> Such a Portia as this generation, at least, has not witnessed—the most joyous and radiant, the most winning and womanly, the most graceful and genial, presentment of the lovely lady of Belmont *Punch* has ever had the delight of applauding—as intense in the tenderness and self-devotion of the part as she is arch and exquisite in its playfulness—as natural in her bye-play as she is true in the feeling, and subtle in the emphasis, with which she delivers its exquisite poetry—in look, movement and utterance, a Portia worthy of **SHAKESPEARE**.[36]

Not only was she likened to a portrait that had stepped down from its frame but also, according to Graham Robertson, she was "*par excellence* the Painter's Actress" who "appealed to the eye before the ear; her gesture and pose were eloquence itself." Criticism like this was unique to Terry, writes Michael Booth: "No performer in the history of the English stage had ever before been considered in quite these pictorial terms"—a consequence of a continuing development in which both production and performer were thought of as works of art as, increasingly, pictorial style dominated the stage.[37]

Descriptions of locations and costumes give some sense of that style, which derives in part from stage directions, many of which copy Kean's text. Knowing that Bassanio's casket choosing took place at "the hall in Portia's palace" sets that scene apart and so invites imagining the location in detail that goes beyond this text's marginal notes: "candles on table, writing materials, sealing wax, dusty box and B pad paper [?]." Godwin designs a diagonal spatial arrangement (also inherited from Kean) for the Belmont scenes and the Trial that pulls the two together. He gives the casket choosing a lavish materiality, with caskets decorated in "damascened work with paneled sides bearing repoussé work of gold or silver" for two of them and "cast work of lead" for the third; he includes Chinese porcelain vases for flowers, lapis lazuli cups, Murano glasses and "*a parrot or some lovebirds in a cage, or on a stand.*"[38] Even minus Godwin's sense of décor, marginalia situating props and blocking performers' positions follow a literal level of annotation seemingly cued as much for a bookholder or prompter as for performers. Only once does a marginal "music" seem potentially more than literal, for it occurs at a moment in Bassanio's casket-choosing where the printed stage direction—"*Music whilst Bassanio comments on the caskets to himself, it then ceases*"—has been reduced to "*Music,*" effectively replacing a precise notation with a generic one.[39] Strike-outs of Jessica's and Lorenzo's parts, reassigned lines and emendations, among them cutting Portia's mention of Bassanio taking her to church and calling her wife, also seem aimed at a bookholder and are indifferently marked, letting one cut stand for many. A further change at the lexical level also has to do with Bassanio's part: as he is about to choose, a marginal "God" replaces "good" in "Some good direct my judgment"; after he discovers Portia's image, "what I *see* be true" replaces "what I *say* be true." Does the latter change simply restore a more authoritative word or, more trenchantly, stress vision or sight—*a propos* to the context? Written-in additions that restore lines deleted from Portia's responses to Bassanio's choice of the lead casket appear across the tops of two adjacent script pages. Although it is difficult to determine who is responsible for cuts, cross-outs and write-ins in an already rearranged script, the written-in material resembles the hand in Hermione's cue-script. The passage in question (echoing Kate's "finale" in *Taming of the Shrew*), keyed into the printed script, begins with "The full sum of me/Is sum of something" and concludes as she "Commits [her spirit] to be directed,/As from her lord, her governor, her king (3.2.157–67)." Did Terry herself ask that these lines be restored? And were they spoken? I would like to think so on both counts, but yet, like much about working with this—or any—rehearsal script, that conjecture stems from a reader's desire.[40]

Bodied spaces

Godwin views the trial not as a fantasy-fiction but as taking place in 1590s Venice; moreover, he suggests, given the "miniature frame" of the Prince of Wales' stage, that it take place in the relatively small Sala dello Scrutinio in the Doge's palace rather than the great Sala del Maggior Consiglio. Matching Belmont's diagonal setting, his scaled-down courtroom features a raised platform for the Doge and dignitaries at stage right and a table set in front of that, around which the action takes place. Not only does he carefully block the positions of Shylock, Antonio, Bassanio, Nerissa and Portia as the action evolves but these moments offer another instance where script and Godwin's scene-setting align in terms of mapping the trial's back-and-forth structure. At the bottom of the page, a crude sketch dovetails perfectly with Godwin's description.[41] Significantly, as though rediscovering and bringing gesture and bodily movement into present presence, a stage direction retains classic business: "(SHYLOCK *kneels on one knee, and whets his knife upon the sole of his shoe)*." Similarly, annotations provide a skimpy list of what appears on the table—the bond, old Bell[ario's] letter, money bags—but as at Belmont, Godwin is infinitely more precise. He imagines "a rich cover of crimson velvet reaching to the floor"; on the table, "the folios of the statutes of Venice with their magnificent bindings and gilded clasps, inkstands of bronze . . . the portfolios of the 'learned doctors', the deed or bond, the knife, the letter from old Bellario and the coffer containing Portia's 9,000 ducats."[42]

If clothes were part of Terry's "greatest effect," a different sort of effect was yet to come. As at the casket-choosing, Portia's wry remarks are written in and keyed to the printed page—"Your wife would give you little thanks for that/If she were by to hear you make the offer"—as are Nerissa's: "'Tis well you offer it behind her back,/The wish would make else a quiet house." The two comments establish several levels of attentiveness onstage: not only do they position Portia and Nerissa as spectators, they also heighten a sense of one-to-one tension. That culminates when, as Portia announces that Shylock may take his pound of flesh but in doing so shed no blood, one annotation reads, "1st sensation in court," followed by a barely legible "2nd sensation"—faded script squeezed into the margins. Acknowledging the presence of onstage spectators, surrogates for an off-stage audience, the moment offers a stunning instance of what might have been called, in 1910s motion pictures, "punch"—that is, the narrative comes to a moment of revelation, a climactic "sensation" that occasions an intense kinesthetic response.[43]

In the first of several end points which are not endings, Bassanio offers Portia three thousand ducats in payment for her lawyer's fee and Antonio speaks of his indebtedness "in love and service evermore." To whom is this directed? Portia, Bassanio, or both? If that depends on performers' choices, a solid horizontal line printed across the page definitively signals "the end." Below it, however, an explanation appears—"*As this Play is sometimes performed in four acts, Dr. Valpy's alteration is inserted here, being that usually adopted*"[44]—but is crossed out. It consists of cod Shakespeare, a near-parodic précis in which Portia and Nerissa reveal their disguises to Bassanio and Gratiano, quickly winding up the comic plot. What follows instead is the scenario of the ring exchange—or, more accurately, *some* of that scenario. For when Portia responds to Bassanio's vow to keep the ring—"That 'scuse serves many men to save their gifts" (4.1.440)—that moment, as well as the entire page, has been decisively and selectively crossed out. One annotation, however, emerges from this confusing stream of markings: on the printed page Gratiano returns the ring to Portia, yet the script has "Ant[onio?]" written over his name, generating an enticing reading in which it is Antonio who gives the disguised Portia her ring (4.2.5–7), effectively bonding the two together—for each has saved the other. Another ending? Again, I would like to think so—and let Terry speak for herself. "Never until I appeared as Portia," she wrote, "had I experienced the feeling of the conqueror. I knew that I had 'got them' when I spoke, 'You see me, Lord Bassanio, where I stand'. 'What can this be?' I thought. '*Quite* this thing has never come to me before! *This is different*'."[45] If the script ends in uncertainty, opening out onto silences and absences, Terry's memory of her performance in the casket choosing provides an apt conclusion by returning to the very first pages of this strange document.

Godfather with daughters: Ian McKellen's King Lear (2007)

In several senses, McKellen's rehearsal script for Lear also is incomplete: six pages are missing; some are dog-eared, tattered, tea- or coffee-stained; and most bear annotations that have been partially or completely erased[46]—evidence of heavy use. Just as outside information clarifies aspects of Terry's Portia script, so too with McKellen's; comparable annotative methodologies also draw the two together across more than a century. Reading McKellen's palimpsestuous *King Lear* script, however, represents a different exercise in interactive dele-ology—a process that tests the limits of digital re-mastering to recuperate and so restore some sense of McKellen's meticulously material theatricality.[47] McKellen's script resembles a performance score; tracking his markings reveals how his voice articulates performance in terms of space and time. Mapping structures of presence and action, of time, timing and times gives these pages a shape and form they do not intrinsically possess but which, at least in part, emerges from the search itself and the time the search takes.[48] Several anecdotes offer a frame, even a theory. I recall, for instance, scratching off the fairies' gossamer draperies on the end papers of my *Blue Fairy Book* in order to see what was underneath. More to the point, in a 1551 woodcut of *Roma*, Leonardo Bufalini overlaid an image of the modern city on a plan of ancient Rome using different shading techniques, making it possible for viewers to compare the ancient and contemporary and reflect on the effects of time.[49]

Playing at codes

At first glance, reading McKellen's script means looking for what's not there, listening for whispers, paying attention to silences. Indeed, his annotations evoke Beckett's idea of failing again, failing better. McKellen consistently "fresh-performs" the words—that is, he self-corrects his performance by infinitesimal shifts in speech, gesture or movement, which may suggest one rationale for the widespread erasures. Some notes that do remain map stage space with a simple X or xx; more precise directions—"to me here!" "More to me," "STOP THIS THUG," "back to chair"—not only chart McKellen's relation to other performers but the commanding tone also may suggest that his Lear is seated, requiring others to come to him. Another strand of marginalia—"NATURALISTIC FOR CAMERA," "picture" and, tied to Lear's last exchange with Fool ("We'll go to supper in the morning" . . . "I'll go to bed at noon" [3.6.81–82]), "pause in shot"—concern playing for the camera. Do McKellen's erasures, then, purposefully eliminate staging directions in order to re-think the performance for filming? If nothing else, remaining annotations acknowledge performance as a disappearing act, imagine rehearsal process (and presence) as a practice forever slipping away. Yet despite that sense of loss, some traces—a heavy line beside a speech, an inked-in addition, a bold **XXX**—convey the force of McKellen's hand on the page, bringing his body into the room as I read.

First beginners

Although the script's initial page goes missing from the cache at the V&A Theatre and Performance archive, bringing forward information from John Lahr's August 2007 interview with McKellen, when he was still playing the role, tracks the tensions of his thinking. "Omnipotent, Dictator, God," glosses Lear's (silent) entrance; from the outset he imagines himself in the storm: "It's his mind that's declining but being woken, and there are explosions happening. There's a storm in his mind."[50] He also kept a typed-out copy of his curse to Cordelia—"Here I disclaim my paternal care,/ Propinquity and property of blood,/ And as a stranger to my heart and me/ Hold them from this forever"—tucked into his dressing-room mirror. Two crises, then, not only preoccupy his consciousness but also shape—and shake—his selfhood. When Lahr asked why he kept this passage before him, McKellen remarked enigmatically, "I'm sure it's to do with having this dreadful repressed secret. . . . Dodging around the central fact, not totally committing."[51]

McKellen's primary scoring strategy entails meticulous underlining, italicizing, adding multiple exclamation points for further emphasis ("But for true need!!!" [2.2.459]) and copying-out—mnemonics reminiscent of John Gielgud's and Ralph Richardson's scripts. Similarly, slashes mark pauses or short breaks; other means of achieving emphasis entail drawing sounds together—"*They durst* not *do* it"; "They *could* not, *would* not, *do* it" (2.2.12–13). "LEAR IS ILL, HOMELESS TIRED" and "not believing it yet" (2.2.290) preface Lear's discovery of Kent in the stocks, and McKellen has copied out his appeal to Gloucester in a scrawled hand on the verso page, emending it (as in Terry's Portia script) with lines that have been crossed through in the playtext. That also is the case with several other passages McKellen has copied out, as though treating the (blank) verso page as a kind of memory bank. Certainly McKellen's approach to Lear's DNA is forensic: not only do his annotations pay unusual attention to process but they also are sensitive to the pyrotechnics of Shakespeare's text, its balance, mass and rhythm, patterns of light and dark, color

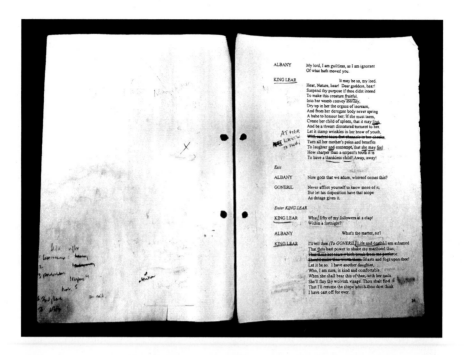

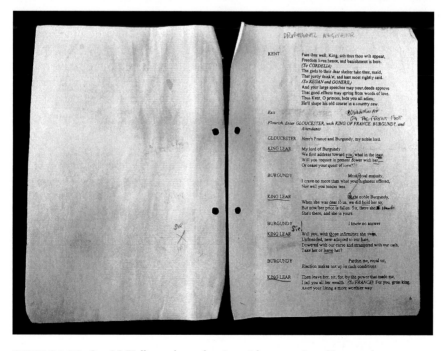

FIGURE 2.2–2.3   Ian McKellen, rehearsal script with annotations. Verso and recto pages. 2007. Victoria and Albert Theatre and Performance Archive. Reproduced by kind permission of Ian McKellen.

and weight, the patina of consonants, the voluptuousness of vowels and their repetitions.[52] Occasionally, notes mark the physical and mental activities associated with his psychological abuse of Goneril—"At her, wanting to hurt"—or, as he appeals to Regan to take his part—"WANT HER CONCERN."

Throughout, marginalia tend to occur within a cluster. McKellen's comments may signal mood or attitude, whether in response to a line, a phrase, a speech, a passage or a developing scenario. For instance, "PROFESSIONAL NEGOTI-ATOR" glosses Lear's responses to Burgundy's and France's suits to Cordelia (1.2. 243–247); similarly, "GODFATHER" not only expresses his sense of self—"Who am I, sir?"; "Who is it that can tell me who I am?" (provoking McKellen's apt "DEADLY JOKES DANGEROUS")—but also comments on the idea of exchanging love for service that weaves throughout the play.

Digital cookery[53]

Consider the following annotations, which appear in the left bottom corner of the verso pages, opposite the finale of Lear's curse on Goneril (a heavily edited version of 1.4.288–302):

I zero in on this passage of annotations because it is unique to this rehearsal script (as well as to others in this chapter), because it brings together several different kinds of marginalia, and it shows what McKellen chooses to keep, what he chooses to erase and what *can* be brought up through digital re-mastering. "**Left**" and "**Right**" presumably indicate Lear's stage moves and position; the list of properties—"**hat**," "**gloves**," "**whip**"—cue both backstage props team and McKellen's Lear as he prepares to exit (a written-in stage direction, repeated on the ensuing page). With the exception of "**Powerlessness**," these annotations, including "**attention**" (written at a slant), seem to float free of the playtext, though numbers stitch a grid pattern, a kind of time machine to moments in McKellen's annotative methodology.

When digitally re-mastered, many more notes become discernable but only partially readable, as with "Master" (at right of notes on stage position) and especially "whipped Goneril once" (bordered, enclosed within a rectangle below "attention,"

	Left		*Right*	
1	[unreadable words]		[blacked out word]	
2			[blacked out word]	
3	Powerlessness			
			1st glove 4	
				attention
		hat 5		
6	2nd glove		on exit	
7	whip			

nearly visible without enhancement)—erasures constituting underwriting, seemingly representing internal thought or memory, that adds fresh ingredients to the recipe. Yet such additions also are particularly frustrating, because adjustments to color exposure, contrast, saturation and sharpness also can tempt readers to translate blurred notes and leap to conclusions, conjecturing the sense of what exists beyond barely discerning two or three letters. Several pages illustrate an exemplary range of effects and affects. In the passage mapping Lear's banishing of Kent and Cordelia (1.1.150—180), a heavily inked-in line joins Kent's "Revoke thy gift" with Lear's echoed response, "This shall not be revoked" (1.1.165; 1.1.180). And in the passages surrounding Kent's release from the stocks (2.2.287–317), McKellen's numbered notes track the developing scenario, hinting at Lear's disintegrating sense of self—"TAKE IT ALL IN—IT DRAGS (?) U OUT," "He's been v angry, but it's mostly his pride (?)," "HE'S SHAKEN OFF" and "not himself" (2.2.315)—which reaches a climax as he kneels before Regan to ask forgiveness, noting "What he's never done before" (2.2.343–345) and posing a question without an answer: "What let her down before." A contradictory "LOSES IT—CONTROL" prefaces Lear's banishment of Goneril from his sight; "TERROR" burrs onto "But yet thou art my flesh, my blood, my daughter" (2.2.410); "NOT WEAK" glosses "You think I'll weep . . . I'll not weep" (2.2.471) and "Continuing tears" attaches to "O Fool, I shall go mad." Some fifty lines later, Lear is in the storm, where McKellen's glosses—"talk to wind" and "be the wind"—imagine him embedded within it.

Final things

Ending as it began, with absence, McKellen's script includes a cluster of fragmentary remains, signaling both a building sense of vocal loss and strongly suggesting that McKellen's Lear continues to monitor verbal performance—those of others as well as his own. What stands for ending occupies two blank pages, the first of which carries a list—"meeting," "draws out (the hovel)," "thou hast little wit," "a pestilent gall to me" and "end play." Cobbling Lear's words together with Fool's—the central doubles act in a play shot through with doubles—maps an arc through the narrative; arguably that points towards the play's Janus-faced texture, its contradictory ability to speak truth to power—and to its lack.

The script's very last page juxtaposes Edgar's "Speak what we feel, not what we ought to say" with a scatter-shot series of self-reminders, which sound like McKellen's rough translation of director's comments or a shorthand version of his own thinking.

> "CLOSE TO ANOTHER"
> "Increase past cushions + [ergo] diction"
> "Clarify idea"
>
> "CARRY C. HIGHER"

I would like to imagine that there is method in capitalizing "CLOSE TO ANOTHER" and "CARRY C. HIGHER," markers of physical movement that frame two subordinate entries—"Increase past cushions + [ergo] diction" and "Clarify idea" (*which* idea, exactly?)—the one calling attention to movement as well as vocal register, the other to mental activity. Might the cushions refer to the location of Goneril's and Regan's bodies? If so, this note reminds McKellen to move past them and to articulate with greater clarity. To attribute meaning to the gap before "CARRY C. HIGHER" insists on Cordelia's physical presence, for the very end of the play is, after all, about her, about anchoring sight with feeling through Lear's signature move. Whether reaching forwards, edging inside or staying in the moment of the curtain call, McKellen glances at what his annotations do and have done throughout: take Shakespeare's playtext beyond itself, say what Lear does not (or cannot) say, set filled time against empty time. How does McKellen's *King Lear* end? With a backstage cheat: "She stands on a chair and I lift her in the wings."[54] We are, after all, in a theatre.

Women's history

Harriet Walter's rehearsal script for Brutus in *Julius Caesar* (2012–2013), separated from Ellen Terry's two scripts by more than a century yet more or less contemporaneous with McKellen's *King Lear* script, resembles the two yet is set apart from both.[55] On the one hand, Walter lightly crosses through every line of her part—echoing codes familiar from other rehearsal scripts that serve to establish ownership and as a means of "being there." On another, her script's organization differs markedly from Terry's or McKellen's scripts. Two framing sections, each thickly inscribed, bracket a central section comprising Shakespeare's playtext adapted for performance.[56] Those pages prefacing the text weave together detailed, often time-identified comments and queries; the final section, linked to a lecture on historical contexts (presumably addressed to the entire cast), documents Walter's notes. The script thus constitutes a memory machine, a storehouse of ideas and texts, sources and resources, textual and artisanal labor,[57] methodologies and marginalia that provide material for further interpretive labor, not just by Walter but also by readers. Implicitly as well as explicitly, textually and through annotations, Walter's script announces that women inmates in a women's prison are rehearsing *Julius Caesar*. A Prologue, crafted from Cassius' speech in which he readies himself for action against Caesar and spoken by three prisoners, aptly defines the inmates' situation: though confined, they vow to "shake off" tyranny "at pleasure."[58] Less formally, selected annotations on the two pages prefacing the playtext key into motive and back story: "Prisoners live with & relate to high stakes, not a cheat if it leads aud. to think about women's history and powerlessness" and "Power violence justice freedom [:] women's voices dealt with big ideas." Walter also records director's notes tailored even more specifically to playing Brutus' part: "Portia—stay down with her, telling her the plot then see the mad dog & clear—put on hoodie and knife"; "get yourself in a position on death (★get rid of knife) that you can get up &

stand over the body in shock & do fate speech from there & down for 'Stop Romans' bring on gloves?" Gender, of course, is central to the entire project: "Are you m. or f.—'the character'—the nature of acting"; answering herself, Walter appears conflicted: "In my head, I'm a man."

Two comments—"motoring scenes—force of <u>voice</u> . . . intention produces body language" and "guardian spirit that drives the body"—forge a double-edged mantra. On the one hand, they describe what annotations *do*, how they participate in a flow of tenses, as past, present and future, or in memory, attention, expectation; on another, they denote how language disciplines the body, others as well as one's own, generating a distinctive kinesthetic sense of bodily movements and location.[59] Both kinds of notations not only map rehearsal process but also act as a multi-layered reserve of historical presences and pressures that play across time and media, marking interventions in history and in past knowledges of history. Yet despite such inclusionary moves, what goes missing may hold the real story—that is, two structuring absences rule Walter's script. One has to do with setting the play in a women's prison; another concerns the material appearing in the framing lecture notes, material upon which performers might draw in order to engage with "being (in the) present."[60]

Ways of seeing[61]

At some point during rehearsals, the cast viewed two films—*A Short Film About Killing* and *Caesar Must Die*—which constitute just such shaping resources, generating further layerings through which past, present and future fuse. *A Short Film About Killing* has three characters—a lawyer who has just passed his exams, a taxi driver and Jacek, a young amoral drifter who murders the taxi driver and is executed; by juxtaposing the two killings, the film sets the idea that private individuals should not kill against the notion that the state may freely kill its subjects. Aside from illustrating the obvious conflict between law and ethics as well as the contradictions built into purely legal reasoning, the tightest connections between the film and Lloyd's *Julius Caesar* have to do with the contours of the prison setting, suggesting that "each of us might be a hair's breadth away from senseless killing," and with pushing viewers towards adopting an ethical attitude to a brutal murder.[62] The more extraordinary film, Paolo and Vittorio Taviani's *Caesar Must Die*,[63] set in Rome's Rebibbia, a maximum security prison, not only lays out a ground plan for the concept driving Lloyd's production but also evokes Peter Weiss's *Marat/Sade*, wherein de Sade directs a play performed by asylum inmates. A performance of Brutus' suicide (in color) frames the rest, shot in austere black and white footage, which the Tavianis considered less realistic than color. The prisoners' sentences for murder, drug dealing and crimes associated with the Mafia or Camorra (revealed as they audition for roles) suggest they are no strangers, as Manohla Dargis writes, to "betrayal, vengeance and power, a knife in the gut and hands washed in blood." What Dargis calls the Tavianis' "elemental condensing" neatly dovetails with the prison setting, "as if the high walls, barred windows and suffocating rooms were manifestations of the characters' states of mind."[64] The Senate, the Forum, the battlefield and, most notably, Caesar's wife Calpurnia, go missing from this spared-down adaptation: aside from Brutus' scene with Portia, women remain an imagined trace: one inmate, running his hand over the plush seat in the auditorium where they will perform, says longingly to himself, "Maybe a woman will sit here."

A number of points enact a fusion between Shakespeare's play and the prisoners' lives so that the two seem inseparable: a prisoner from Naples, for instance, remarks that Shakespeare must have walked the streets of his city, not those of Rome; the requiems over Caesar's body take place in the exercise yard with inmates at surrounding windows acting as the crowd; when Mark Antony (Antonio Frasca) speaks of "men of honor," he talks the language of the mob. Salvatore Striano, who plays Brutus, has returned to prison from an acting career to participate in the *Julius Caesar* project; he parallels Walter's Brutus, also a senior cast member: whereas Striano seems to be a general consultant, several fragmentary annotations—among them "CAESURA"; "New thought at full stop (& other punctuation)"—hint that Walter may have moonlighted as a voice coach. At the film's end, the prisoners seem liberated by performing—as did the lifer Rick Cluchey when he played Vladimir in the legendary performance of *Waiting for Godot* in the former Gallows room in San Quentin California State Prison.[65] That moment fades, however, as the guards turn the keys, locking each prisoner in. Once in his cell, lying in bed reading his script, the inmate playing Cassius (Cosimo Rega) remarks, "Since I have discovered art, this cell has turned into a prison"—an idea which resonates with the Prologue: "So every bondman in his own hand bears/The power to cancel his captivity."

Historical gossip

By contrast, the pages following Walter's adapted script gather up material that enacts an historical fusion, largely through the selectivity of her account of an impromptu lecture by Robert Harris, an historian and political journalist for the BBC, fleshing out shifts in politics and attitudes towards democracy at various points during Caesar's rule. "German nineteenth-century historians pro-Nietsche [*sic*] rehabilitated Caesar on the grounds that he brought democracy to the Western hemisphere; once Caesar was destroyed, democracy did not re-appear for 1,800 years." Harris also evokes fairly recent histories and historical figures (other tyrannical rulers or megalomaniacs), pointing to a number of contradictions in Caesar's position on democracy—"strength of spirit cannot be confined—tyranny; no free speech, no elections, imprisonment"—the flip side of his move to censor free speech. He calls Caesar a proto-Hitler or Napoleon ("a charming psychopath") and compares the conspirators to Claus von Stauffenberg (who led a 1944 plot to assassinate Hitler and remove the Nazi party from power). As for Brutus, Harris calls him a lawyer (a term Walter repeats) and considers him politically naïve—"not Mr. Clean; pompous, up to his neck in corruption . . . a prototype Hamlet who has the love of the people, Brutus has 'loser' written all over him—the vacillator 'staring oblivion in the face'."

Actions

Overall, Walter's self-notes together with the materials compiled on the framing pages write the history of designing a role and negotiating its surrounding world through linking motion, e-motion and action.[66] In that regard, this script's most revealing form of marginalia is actioning—an annotative process that marks the physical and mental activities associated with a single line that describe what a character wishes *to do to* the character with whom she/he speaks, using transitive verbs, the most "doing" of the doing verbs.[67] This array of precise, concrete actions attached to words focuses attention on what the language does, keeping the drama active.[68] Also figuring in this process are words that explicitly connect to the body's actions—grasp, pull, lift—and to its movements as well as to concepts indicating the structure of action or events (starting, stopping, resuming), including those having to do with process or with a process completed.

How, then does a rehearsal script "capture the texture and timing of bodies in motion, transpose the moved in the direction of the written"—that is, how does a script view the body as a choreographer might, as capable of generating ideas—a "bodily writing" that enables, as Susan Leigh Foster writes, character, kinesthesia and empathy to construct corporeality in a given historical and cultural moment?[69] More directly, what does actioning make comprehensible on paper? To what does it give access? Potentially, actioning, which locks Shakespeare's words into a kind of prison house of language (in several senses of that phrase), risks "verbal over-shadowing"—arguably a process that inhibits imaginative responses—that is, where verbal reasoning replaces the imaginative stimuli that follow perceptual pathways, resulting in *over*-staging the text.[70] In order to avoid that stricture, actioning can be thought of as merging the phenomenal and the semiotic body and, as with McKellen's script, viewing mind as *em-bodied* and body as *en-minded*, Erika Fischer-Lichte's elegant condensation that collapses any strict distinction between body and mind, the physical and the psychological, working on a role from the outside in or from the inside out.[71]

Parting Brutus; or actioning in action

Walter explores Brutus' role through what she refers to as his rhetoric of waiting and watching: naming tentativeness her "default setting" for "finding the character, the prison persona," she speaks of reaching for and grabbing at anything close and present that will feed into her thinking about a scene or gloss a line. Here, the concept of presence poses the question of a scene—the body-subject (that is, the phenomenal body) and the body-object (the semiotic body), the player and the dramatic figure, are inextricably bound up with each other.[72] Using present-day idiom—as, when the battle nears, Brutus hears of Portia's death, "BRING IT ON—WIN FOR PORTIA'S SAKE"—gives a line "punch," that is, a moment when the narrative reaches a revelation that occasions an intense kinesthetic response.[73] Shards of sentences mark other moments that capture the gist of a scene: "Casca describes the police state"; "P insists on being B's equal"; "BLOKES AT BAR"; "Warlords in suits, carry guns, etc."; "The assassins welcome freedom"; "MACHO FACE OFF" (Brutus and Mark Antony meet)—or a speech— "INAUGURAL" (Brutus' speech following the assassination). The audience, remarks Walter, "should be left with expectation that B is the next visionary leader."

Walter's glosses for Brutus' initial soliloquy, titled IF HE'S KING, illustrate a representative range of marginalia, corresponding to 3.1.146ff. in a modern text: adding "They say tomorrow/The senators mean to establish Caesar as a king" and "3 AM" to mark fictional time; framing Brutus' time-bound obsession: "Not psychologically sequential; Compressing time/no time; the lawyer." Two other temporal signatures—"The audience have just said 'There has to be another way'" and "9/11"—call attention to recent events, inside as well as outside the fiction. Both echo Cassius' prophetic sense that Caesar's assassination already has become the stuff of history: "How many ages hence/Shall this our lofty scene be acted over/In states unborn and accents yet unknown"—positioning Walter's Brutus not just as one more iteration of the role but also as an uncanny re-enactment.[74] "9/11" ties more explicitly to Walter's desire to reach for present-day instances that will resonate with Caesar's past history, bringing both freshly alive, present in memory and imagination.

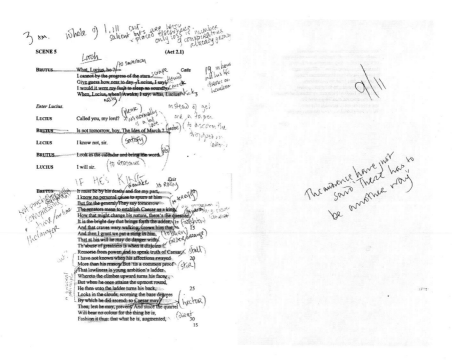

FIGURE 2.4 Harriet Walter, rehearsal script with annotations. Verso and recto pages. 2011–2012. Reproduced by kind permission of Harriet Walter.

Being before

The fragmentary voices I have been listening to oscillate between thought and doing, rehearsing and reflecting, memory and performance, enacting self-performative gestures—a double perspective of movement and rest that hints at how players spend energy over the course of a scene. These scripts perform as witnesses: looking at them, I imagine that I touch the real[75]—the flashes and flares of a past theatrical life. As I turn to Antony Sher's rehearsal scripts, held in his private archive, I'm aware that not only is there a different sense of being there at Sher's generous invitation but also, when returning to my study, I see that nearly every photographed page bears an image of my fingers, registering my hands-on experience (leaving my DNA behind) of discerning the minutiae and contingencies of his private reading practice. Most of the annotative strategies and mnemonics already mentioned also mark Antony Sher's rehearsal scripts, which he previously has mined in *The Year of the King*, in essays in *Players of Shakespeare 2* and *5* and in *Beside Myself*[76]—writing that aligns with Jerome McGann's views of the socialization of a work as it passes from rehearsal to performance.[77] Extensively glossed and annotated, adorned with images, they capture some sense of the suspended indecisiveness characterizing that process where interpretive possibilities remain contingent, in flux, even through previews and shifts from Stratford's main stage to London's

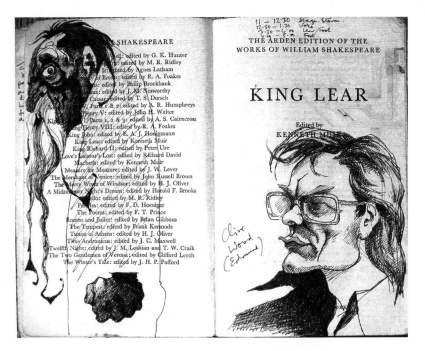

FIGURE 2.5 Antony Sher, drawing of King Lear. Rehearsal script with annotations. Reproduced by kind permission of Antony Sher. Photograph © Richard Abel.

Barbican. They also record a more private discourse in which Sher talks to himself—or, better, speaks with his avatars: Lear's Fool, Richard III, Shylock, Macbeth. Setting any one of the previous rehearsal scripts beside a page from one of Sher's scripts, heavy with immediacy, highlights just how unusual the latter are. Aides memoire, user's manuals, commonplace books, sketchbooks, actor's variorums: these are *embodied* books—proxies that trace voice and body, relations between bodies and theatrical time and timing. "The actor," writes Sher, "is a portrait painter—of others and of himself."[78] Writes John Berger, "The practice of drawing touches or is touched by something prototypical and anterior to logical reasoning. . . . It is a form of probing [deriving] from the human need to plot points, to place things and place oneself"[79]—marking-up as a physical substitution exercise.

Fooling

To begin with, Sher's script for *King Lear*'s Fool. One image sketches Lear's profile (see Figure 2.5), his right hand cramped into a cruel fist, the anger or determination it holds rising from the page. Other pages of Sher's scripts feature depictions of the fool, such as an oddly abstract image of a face in profile atop an outlined body, made from squiggles that warp the image, which owes a debt to Dali and to the surrealists' interest in how automatic drawing articulates the id and dreams; as Francis Bacon says of his paintings of the Eumenides, this is hardly a literal portrait but rather represents the effect that Lear, or a combination of Lear and Gloucester, has on the viewer—evoking the sense that the artist has peeled back layers of skin and uncovered flesh. Sher's Richard III script incorporates snippets of historical-theatrical gleanings, sound bytes from conversations with directors, designers, voice coaches and company members, word frequency and critical contexts (material similar to that in Harriet Walter's script for Brutus in *Julius Caesar*)—"end of medieval world; Renaissance: humanism, doubt, curiosity"; "mouths of hell and heaven"; "common words: God, Lord; most used word: Guilt"; "Can see him either as Anti-Christ or as man in search of soul."

I weave through Sher's scripts, attentive to what he lingers on, ignores, repeats, hurries towards, inches away from, brings together—as though in a dance.[80] Doing so, I re-envision Sher's choices and winnowings, creating a fiction of his autobiographical turn. Listening to a specialist reader who is doubly self-conscious, marking a role's self-signs and the rehearsals of self that shape his ownership of the role, does not just reveal what the actor's presence does *to* the text but also enables a reader to locate theoretically two bodies in one: the body producing (that of the actor) and the body produced (that of the character).[81] In short, annotation functions as a transformative practice that re-authorizes the play's textual status: no longer does its literary value or consciousness have primacy. When, in *Shakespeare in Love*, Shakespeare summarizes the story of "Romeo and Ethel the Pirate's Daughter" for the assembled cast, Hugh Fennyman, the production's money man, asks Tilney, the Master of Revels, "Who is that?" "Never mind," responds Tilney, writing Shakespeare out of equation, "Nobody. The author." As Bert States writes,

Shakespeare's text has become a theatrical document keyed to the "hovering self of the actor as the character passes through him."[82]

Significantly, not only do margins become a metaphor for challenges to otherwise closed systems of philosophy and writing in general but the power of margins and white space also becomes harnessed to re-figuring presence—following a rhetoric of process, something that occurs with an all-at-once-ness, a mash-up of annotative forms and functions, a repository of intellectual, emotional and physical life oscillating at particular moments in time. Often, drawings obey no logical plan but seem randomly positioned, keyed to filling available white space with sketches, exploratory thoughts or suggestions for future improvements. Yet at other times, image, annotation or both together connect with a passage to reveal an uncanny eruption of a theatrical unconscious, "mak[ing] something visible but also accompany[ing] something invisible to its incalculable destination."[83] What Benjamin called the optical unconscious is not revealed through photography: if it

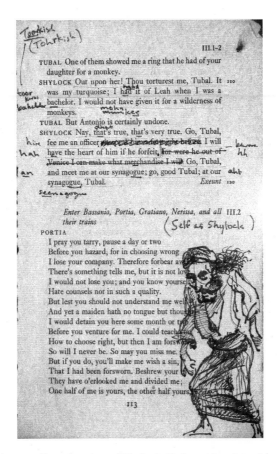

FIGURE 2.6 Antony Sher, drawing of Shylock. Rehearsal script with annotations. Reproduced by kind permission of Antony Sher. Photograph © Richard Abel.

can be spoken of at all as externalized in the visual field, that is because it is constructed there by the viewer. In such metamorphoses of reading, the relations between performer and spectator occur as traces of suspended time, connected to memory and to how we imagine or remember events, feelings, sensations.

As I encounter them, Sher's drawings are performances: at such moments of interplay, his script becomes a serendipitous theatre of encounter, a paper stage for performances that encompass varied horizons of legibility and intelligibility.[84] As a visual image encroaches upon a passage, physicality is never very far away, hovering just out of sight, at times with astonishing effects. Shylock appears beside Portia's "I pray you tarry, pause a day or two/Before you hazard": his figure, and his own impending trial, extend beyond his meeting with Tubal to haunt Bassanio's casket-choosing; Portia's fair flesh aligning with Antonio's brings into view a passing temporal configuration wherein, as Benjamin writes, "what has been comes together in a flash with the now to form a constellation."[85]

"In a glossy margin, Narcissus saw his face"

Creating a radically unstable palimpsest, Sher's marginalia offer flashbacks, turnings and re-turnings, providing what Valéry models as a "continuous commentary, a succession of *notes* escaping from the inner voice.... notes of pure *thought* [that] can haunt us—like passing words overheard in the street, all the more precious because the context remains unknown." Valéry's central image for the place of consciousness "consists of an invisible box in the darkness of a theater—Plato's cave or a coffin—where night hides all the spectators from view, and only the stage of appearances can be seen."[86] Above all, Sher lives in the margins and white spaces, spaces where the unconscious travels into view, especially if and when discoveries made in rehearsal reach into performance. "I wonder," he writes, "if audiences always saw what we had in rehearsal."[87] And just as Gaston Bachelard found compressed time in the spaces of the house, Sher's annotations reveal a similar intensification, an experience of thickened time, of spatial density, generating an awareness of the materiality of time, of the textual world reshaped by intellectual, emotional, psychological and physical energies oscillating at particular moments, reviving and amplifying a sense of performance in its multiple, unsettled possibilities.[88] Not surprisingly, what's marked—or unmarked—shifts from script to script, as though each playtext not only makes certain demands on readers but also invites and/or is open to particular strands of thinking, processes of reflection that shape marginalia on the play they supplement. Also apparent is a curious sense of connection among several roles—Fool, Richard, Macbeth. Fear of injury joins Fool to Richard; Richard as child-killer connects him to Macbeth. A series of time capsules, swerves of duration, snapshots of what's in mind: these traces are stacked in no chronological order, shifting between figure and ground. Entries bearing "real-time" signatures for run-throughs, dress rehearsals, previews or "self-notes" edge towards performance, enable tracking how Sher wrests authorial control from Shakespeare, diminishing his voice, as though to say, with Coriolanus, "I'll stand as if a man were author of himself..."

FIGURE 2.7 Richard "woos" Lady Anne. Penelope Beaumont (standing in for Anne) and Antony Sher in rehearsal. Royal Shakespeare Company Collection. 1984. Photograph © Reg Wilson.

Dancing the argument

That is especially apparent with *Richard III*, where annotations for the so-called wooing of Lady Anne reconsider and re-figure modes of action and behavior and, as in a rare rehearsal photograph, call attention to the body's enunciations in space. The scene relies upon thinking through established codes of conduct between female and male bodies: where the body of one sex can touch the body of the other, what kinds of shapes the two sexes can make together, who can give weight and who can bear it, who initiates movement and who follows, who is passive and who active, who is to be looked at and who is doing the looking.[89] Against an empty conference-hall backdrop, the more intimate backdrop is a high-backed choir stall, standing in for the coffin with Henry VI's corpse, papers and a crumpled cloth on its seat. Penelope Beaumont's Lady Anne stands apart at left frame, arms crossed across her chest, as if to protect herself; Sher's Richard, his lips caressing the staff in his hands, leans toward her from right frame, balanced awkwardly on the arm rest, his right leg given less weight than the left, so that the image sets his deformity and his abjectly pleading upward glance against Anne's tall, self-composed figure. A cluster of Sher's annotations offer a parallel of their encounter: "divine perfection of [a] woman—genuine, just keep steady at her"; "better for that place—genuine/I believe in it as much as you"; "Lady Anne—sword (if thy revengeful heart cannot forgive) NEW THOUGHT"; "wet his grave with my repentant tears—MORE GENUINE"; "was ever woman in this humour wooed—faster getting back to audience"—or suggest microscopic shifts in verbal emphasis—"study <u>fashions</u> to adorn my <u>body</u>."[90] On the one hand, Sher thinks as the character, mouths his words—"divine perfection of a woman"; on the other, he re-marks his physical behavior—"genuine, just keep steady at her" (a Stanislavskian riff, reminding him of a larger strategy lest he get too caught up in the tactics). Do these, I wonder, represent instances of the monomania tied to Richard's role, its powerful tug on the actor, usurping his subjectivity, enfolding one agency within another?

Penny Downie's Lady Anne, her white-painted face framed in black, seems to preside over, even control, the wooing scene. However, a note—"We associate grief-stricken people with being good. Is she?"—complicates that reading, as does Figure 2.9, where her figure, arms raised high, suggests her openness; an offhand joke—"Having trouble with your pallbearers, love?"—negotiates the interface between role and player, further signaling her vulnerability. Yet another note— "curses linked to praying; perverted form of avenging God"—pulls into viewing her as a harpy, a revenger; following that thread nets in Christopher Ravenscroft's Richmond, whose head, jutting chin and extended neck replicate Downie's features, joining the two as anti-Richard figures. Do these whitened faces derive from Sher's fascination with Stephen Dwoskin's film of himself, severely crippled with polio, propped on crutches, extending a hand to touch "a semi-naked woman, bathed in cool white light, her skin like porcelain against her black hair; his own hand turning from black to white as it enters the light, attempting to touch her but without making contact?"[91]

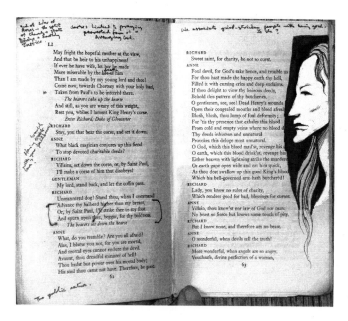

FIGURE 2.8 Antony Sher, drawing of Lady Anne (1). Rehearsal script with annotations. Reproduced by kind permission of Antony Sher. Photograph © Richard Abel.

FIGURE 2.9   Antony Sher, drawing of Lady Anne (2). Rehearsal script with annotations. Reproduced by kind permission of Antony Sher. Photograph © Richard Abel.

Talking the talk

Each script, of course, engages with this confluence of role and actor, invites negotiations that shape marginalia. Although most reveal how annotation thickens time and space in relation to *physical* behaviors, two follow different patterns: one grafts predominantly to language, the other maps structures of unvoiced thought. In choosing to play Shylock as a Levantine Jew, Sher not only was tying character to early modern historicity but also re-positioning himself as slightly alien to his own ethnicity. As he singles out particular lines—"Hath not a Jew eyes? (CAN'T A JEW SEE WHAT'S GOING ON?)"; "if [his flesh] will feed nothing else, it will feed my revenge; <u>NB</u>: Before, he said man's flesh was useless"—a reader becomes unusually aware of how responsive writing promotes a sense of intimacy as he worries through re-staging words, fine-tuning the soundscape of his performance through sonic remixing or sampling. Precisely marked to carry a sense of consonantal rush, of pulled-out, extended vowel sounds, an entire stereophony re-crafts the grain of the voice, translating Shakespeare to ape the accents of Levantine Jewry—pre-performative work that echoes the orality of performance practice.

Finding the look

For Macbeth, Sher's annotations excavate the mind's depths, bringing its cries and whispers to the surface. Pasted onto the script's first page, an image of an infant

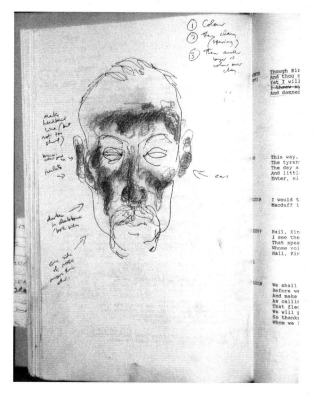

FIGURE 2.10 Antony Sher, drawing of Macbeth's face, with annotations. Reproduced by kind permission of Antony Sher. Photograph © Richard Abel.

"frozen, white, wearing an embroidered shift, lying in a tiny plank-and-nail coffin."[92] Captioned "Our baby," it offers a defining frame for marginalia that resemble a therapist's scenario for scenes from a marriage: "They've had a child who's died; a tragedy in the family. Whose fault?" "Why is Mac fighting like 'berserker' (that is, blacking out, hardly conscious)? To make sure the others don't get crown? Because of marriage?" "Do they argue—fight? Yes, probably." "Feedback loop to one another; they think, speak and suffer together." And the Macbeth baby haunts their marriage: at "If 'twere done when 'tis done" (retitled "Cold Feet" à la Brecht), "Their dead baby?" glosses "And Pity, like a naked new-born babe ..." "Waking one another with nightmares; stopping sleeping together." "When he cuts her off, is he worried she's going to make him more anxious? Does he hate the idea she knows what he did (in the dark); guilt and shame?" Sher's choice to gloss the Lady's reading of Macbeth's letter—"This letter written between witches and Forres SC; a kind of love letter; she doesn't know Mac has been named successor or that King is coming here"—also affirms the couple's interdependence. No image of "Self as Macbeth" (as in his *Lear* script) appears: Sher writes, "His face isn't important. What lies behind it is. His brain"; he speaks of Macbeth as obsessed with time, as "a man with an existential headache," a "thinking part: the inside of his head races and leaps faster than any show-off on crutches." A sketch of Macbeth's mask-like face detailing instructions for make-up sits opposite Malcolm's closing speech; haunting the ending, trapping the play between child and father, both dead.

Getting over the hump; or "don't break a leg!"

Each script not only reveals particular structures of thought (albeit unconsciously or by their absences) but also connects roles: concern over physical safety joins Sher's performance as Lear's Fool, during which he sustained an incapacitating injury, to Richard III's legendary deformities. Notes obsessed with embodiment trace through Sher's *Richard III* script. What does his body look like? What is the extent of deformity? For Sher, his initial attempt was a kind of fort-da move towards and away from the bodies (and voices) of other actors—Olivier and Ramaz Chividaze from the Rustaveli Company—bodies that worked to block his own. A jokey "Crutches and Hunches" cues the decision to use crutches: Could a disabled man excel as a warrior? Shakespeare, after all, suggests an answer: "A horse, a horse, my kingdom for a horse."[93] In this regard, consider Michael Chekhov's technique of the "imaginary body":

> Try to imagine what kind of body your character might have . . . you will see that . . . the imaginary body of your character is different from yours. Observe this body for a while and then just step into this body . . . what will be the psychological result of such a meeting? You will not and do not need to force yourself to speak differently and move differently. 3 elements: character, imaginary body and your own body.[94]

Were crutches the safest way of playing extreme disability? That issue gathers up several histories of obsession, haunted by competing memories and counter-memories. One, neatly encapsulated in Sher's etching of Richard as a "bottled spider," shows him caught between physical performance and textual alliance. Richard's weight leans forward onto the crutches; flying out behind him, his legs are tethered towlines of ink connecting his figure to "Now is the winter of our discontent made glorious summer by this son of York." Behind Olivier's voice, of course, lies Gielgud's, "true" owner of the Shakespearean sound, to which Sher, conscious of his South African vocal identity, felt barred from access. Confessing his addiction to "the casual dress of flesh" (a line from Rostand's *Cyrano*, a role Sher had played) Sher laments, "If only you could do with the *text* what you can do with the body."[95] The difficulty of doing so is perhaps best illuminated by setting Sher's sense of Olivier's indelible shape beside his own crude micrograph of Richard's bundled hump and spindly crutch, tucked into a corner of the script just as Richard turns Margaret's curse back against her. Yet if Olivier also owned Richard's body, Sher's fascination with physical disguise and commitment to

FIGURE 2.11 Antony Sher's etching of Richard as a "bottled spider." Reproduced by kind permission of Antony Sher. Photograph © Carol Chillington Rutter.

physical excess mark him as Olivier's heir. When, on the last night of the Barbican run, Roger Howells, the RSC's unofficial historian, responsible for organizing Sher's titanium crutches, stole away one crutch to his Stratford shed (what else hides in *this* private archive?), it became a possession, in two senses of the word—for as Alice Rayner writes, "to possess something is also to be possessed by it." Further, to have a material trace that once belonged to another is concretely to feel the other: sharing Sher's struggle to avoid physical injury, Howells affirmed his own part in the saga of fashioning the signature properties that not only would re-define Richard's role for a generation but also would become the most eloquent signs of his physical authority.[96] Potent objects, extensions of body and psyche, the crutches are to Sher's Richard III what the madeleine is to Proust.

Red noses: material Fool

Articulating embodiment for Sher's earliest RSC role, Fool in *King Lear*, took a different form. Keen to avoid copycatting the "little cheeky-chappie jester" of theatrical tradition, Sher amassed an archive of figures—cripples, amputees, paralytics, dwarfs, hunchbacks, freaks, the blind and deformed—and a list of properties—cowl, skirt, bells, scepter or bauble with his own head—accouterments of the

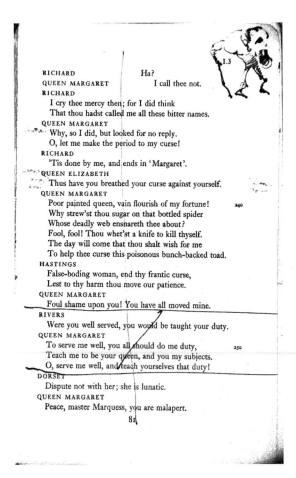

RICHARD   Ha?
QUEEN MARGARET   I call thee not.
RICHARD
  I cry thee mercy then; for I did think
  That thou hadst called me all these bitter names.
QUEEN MARGARET
  Why, so I did, but looked for no reply.
  O, let me make the period to my curse!
RICHARD
  'Tis done by me, and ends in 'Margaret'.
QUEEN ELIZABETH
  Thus have you breathed your curse against yourself.
QUEEN MARGARET
  Poor painted queen, vain flourish of my fortune!   240
  Why strew'st thou sugar on that bottled spider
  Whose deadly web ensnareth thee about?
  Fool, fool! Thou whet'st a knife to kill thyself.
  The day will come that thou shalt wish for me
  To help thee curse this poisonous bunch-backed toad.
HASTINGS
  False-boding woman, end thy frantic curse,
  Lest to thy harm thou move our patience.
QUEEN MARGARET
  Foul shame upon you! You have all moved mine.
RIVERS
  Were you well served, you would be taught your duty.
QUEEN MARGARET
  To serve me well, you all should do me duty,   250
  Teach me to be your queen, and you my subjects.
  O, serve me well, and teach yourselves that duty!
DORSET
  Dispute not with her; she is lunatic.
QUEEN MARGARET
  Peace, master Marquess, you are malapert.
                            81

FIGURE 2.12 Antony Sher, sketch of Richard III. Rehearsal script with annotations. Reproduced by kind permission of Antony Sher. Photograph © Richard Abel.

working entertainer. The key to Fool's physicality, however, was a red nose. "No Ideas but in Things," writes William Carlos Williams: the red nose spawned an entire "Thing World"—bowler hats, a wig, soiled white gloves, a tattered tailcoat, a tiny Suzuki violin, elongated shoes emphasizing Fool's disability, the feet and knees turned inwards—tactile objects comprising an "archive of detritus," blurring lines between play and not-play, mimicking memory—all stored away in the RSC Collection—as the crutch is not.[97] At least four images of "Self as Fool" document Sher's obsession with constructing his presence, ranging from a bundle of inchoate flesh, to sketches increasingly attuned to capturing Fool's attitudes in space: in each, the red nose organizes and grabs attention, whether stretched to phallic proportions or resembling a lollypop. It is as though the impulse to draw is generated by the desire to get closer and closer, to enter the self of what is being drawn.[98]

FIGURE 2.13   Richard III's crutch. Collection of Roger Howell, Stratford-upon-Avon.
Photograph © Helen Hargest.

Micrographies

Annotations from the second run-through and the last preview's self notes record
bodily trades and transfers, inter-relations of body and language, reflect on the
limits of verbal and physical performance, test strategies for shaping modes of
attention, clarify temporal micro-differences. "Beware of prankishness. Know
when to shut up; his lethal cutting edge: political satire"; "violin: play like a mad
thing, part of his pain"; "end of first song: as Lear interrupts savagely; Fool's
(unvoiced) reply: 'Oh, I'm terribly happy, aren't we all?'" Further comments nail
down or alter timing: "egg: deft + fast; don't play for reaction"; "play more boldly
on Goneril exit—don't exclude." Verging closest to performance—as he anato-
mized Regan in the hovel, Lear stabbed Sher's Fool through a cushion—Sher
prescribes that scenario: "pillow might be thrown on 'Bless thy five wits' if I'm in
bin by then or not. For death blow: after King, Kent and Gloucester exit, CLOCK
GLOUCESTER—settle into position with head above rim; on Tom's 'Lurk',
tumble back into bin completely."

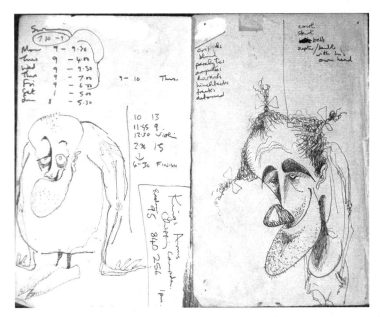

FIGURE 2.14–2.15 Antony Sher, drawings of Self as Fool. Rehearsal script. Reproduced by kind permission of Antony Sher. Photograph © Richard Abel.

FIGURE 2.16 The Fool, Self Portrait, Stratford, 1982 (oil on canvas), Sher, Antony (b.1949). Royal Shakespeare Company Collection, Stratford-upon-Avon, Warwickshire/Bridgeman Images.

Mirrored possession

In ending with Sher's painting, "The Fool, 1982," a "shot" taken from the moments where Fool speaks the prophecy listing the preposterous impossibilities of a world turned topsy-turvy, what I witness is a body caught in the act, an act that is a forgery—an event that never happened, was never adequately witnessed, blending into a future that cannot arrive. As I look, the image threatens to escape the canvas, accompanied by a burst of sound from Ilona Sekacz's "Voice of the Storm," viewed as an additional character, not simply as background accompaniment, which propelled Fool back onstage after Lear, Kent and Gloucester's exit, spinning him into a crazy-cartwheeling dance, ending in a fall (proleptic of his death?). And as I am drawn into its force field, the painting becomes dynamically activated: the figure looking at the viewer, the viewer looking back become active participants.[99] There's the memory of another watcher inscribed in the painting: in the upper left corner, three women watch this scene. Yet if this painting imitates performance, it is not performance per se but a two-dimensional map of performance re-played, an event that enables Fool to re-strut his stuff. Is this something akin to what Benjamin means by the optical unconscious—that moment where layers of perception, co-created by the painting and the field of vision, begin to detach themselves from the painting and float closer to the viewer, setting up a relation between one perception and another that suddenly seems uncanny? Just as I am drawn into its force field, the painting returns my gaze, lurches towards me, laughs back. The memory of Sher's performance—his as well as mine—is held here, its time and timing marked in a different register, conveying a sense of the peculiar capacity of performance to grow in many directions, to entangle with itself, to be simultaneously past and present. Not only is Sher's painting seductive in the way that all elegant performances seduce the viewer but still-stopping his figure enters a time-space warp where cabaret or vaudeville's stand-up comedian comes into view—intensely familiar, distinctively modern—looking ahead to look back (or is it vice versa?), conflating past, present and future. Writes Richard Preiss, "the prophecy is a show-stopper, a moment that literally stops the show as a coherent, time-bound transaction that erases barriers between performer and spectator."[100] All is very precisely keyed to the seventy sound cues of Sekacz's "Voice of the Storm," scored for horns, bass drum, two strings, cymbals, siren, tam tams and whistles, which breaks the prophecy's final sentence into two-to-three-word segments— **"This prophecy   Merlin shall make   for I live   before his time"**— effectively echoing that lack of coherence, as does Sher's vocal performance, to reinforce, in these shared moments, a trace of suspended time, connected to how we imagine or remember events, feelings and sensations. The painting remembers how watchers witnessed the first moments of performance from the upper-right window; once animated, now empty, it awaits another looker-on. Such looking generates an immediacy, what Benjamin calls the "still real"—that is, the future subsists not just *in* the painting but *through* the viewer who discovers it as still, in the sense of still remaining, thus "suspending the onlooker between performance history, the archive and the immediate now."[101] And in a kind of mirrored possession, by bringing material remains into view, touching them, one touches time—and memory—in the register of the senses—time that is not separate from a script, an object or a painting but incorporated within the present—"They are with me, there and here."

Notes

1 H.J. Jackson, *Marginalia: Readers Writing in Books* (New Haven, CT: Yale University Press, 2001). See also Lawrence Lipking, "The Marginal Gloss," *Critical Inquiry* 3.4 (1977), 609–611, and Jacques Derrida, who views margins as a metaphor for challenges to the otherwise closed systems of philosophy and writing in general—*Margins of Philosophy*, trans. Alan Bass (Brighton: Harvester Press, 1982).

2 Farge, *The Allure of the Archives*, trans. Thomas Scott-Railton (New Haven, CT: Yale University Press, 2013), 82.

3 I borrow Asynith Palmer's phrase.

4 See W.W. Greg, *Two Elizabethan Stage Abridgements: The Battle of Alcazar & Orlando Furioso: An Essay in Critical Bibliography* (Oxford: Clarendon Press, 1923), esp. 135. See also David Bradley, *From Text to Performance in the Elizabethan Theatre: Preparing the Play for the Stage* (Cambridge: Cambridge University Press, 1992) (Bradley calls this document "Edward Alleyn's acting scroll," 4, 25); and Simon Palfrey and Tiffany Stern, *Shakespeare in Parts* (Oxford: Oxford University Press, 2007).

5 Farge, *Allure*, 16.

6 See Freddie Rokem, *Philosophers and Thespians: Thinking Performance* (Redwood City, CA: Stanford University Press, 2010), 183, 186. See also Tiffany Stern, "Actors and Parts," in *The Oxford Handbook to Early Modern Theatre*, ed. Richard Dutton (Oxford: Oxford University Press, 2009), esp. 502–503. On grammar-school students' rhetorical practices, see Carol Chillington Rutter, *Shakespeare's Lost Boys on Stage and Screen* (London and New York: Routledge, 2007) and Lynne Enterline, *Shakespeare's Schoolroom: Rhetoric, Discipline, Emotion* (Philadelphia, PA: University of Pennsylvania Press, 2012).

7 See James Boaden's *Memoirs of the Life of John Philip Kemble, esq., including a History of the Stage from the Time of Garrick to the Present Period* (London, Longman, Hurst, Rees, Orme, Brown and Green, 1825), 1.90; and John Taylor, *Records of My Life* (New York: J. & J. Harper, 1833), 270 (full text available online). Judith Pascoe cites Kemble in *The Sarah Siddons Audio Files* (Ann Arbor, MI: University of Michigan Press, 2011), 81. After working with John Barton on verse-speaking, Patrick Stewart remembers underlining half the words during a first session and in the next underlining the other half—see *The Shakespeare Sessions* DVD (Working Arts Library, Denver Center for the Performing Arts, Applause Theatre and Cinema Books, n.d.).

8 *Bingo* is listed as MS 81343 in the John Gielgud Archive, British Library.

9 For the idea of an authoritative archive, see Matthew Reason, "Archive or Memory? The Detritus of Live Performance," *New Theatre Quarterly* 19.1 (2003), 86; see also Eugenio Barba, "Four Spectators," *The Drama Review* (*TDR*) 34.1 (1990), 97.

10 The British Library—shelfmark SCB10 H8 (BL Loan MS 125/64 8SC7 H 1)—notes that it is "in ET's hand." Comparing the annotations on Terry's *Macbeth* script to the cue script's handwriting suggests their similarity. Yet since hands may differ, all that can be said with certainty is that whoever wrote Hermione's part wrote it for Ellen Terry.

11 Act, scene and line numbers refer to *The Winter's Tale*, ed. John Pitcher, Arden 3 edition (London: Methuen Drama, 2010).

12 Tree's version also bowed to the Victorian/Edwardian taste for pictorialism and spectacle. Max Beerbohm recalls seeing a "woodland glade with shepherd's cottage and a babbling brook." On pictorial stagings, see, for instance, Michael R. Booth, *Victorian Spectacular Theatre 1850–1910* (London: Routledge & Kegan Paul, 1981).

13 At the Royal Shakespeare Company, Hermione was not seen as visibly pregnant until 1969, when Judi Dench played the role.

14 Hermione's lines encompass a 25-line passage wherein she mourns being separated from her son and denied childbed privilege (3.2.77–80, 89–114, 117–121); the selection omits her defense of Camillo.

15 Terry would have been familiar with Mamillius' part: in 1856, at the age of eight, she had played the role—her first Shakespearean part—in Charles Kean's company. *A Midsummer Night's Dream*'s Puck and *King John*'s Prince Arthur followed over the next several years: the three roles comprise her repertoire as a child actor, and her casting in *King John* may explain why the folder with Hermione's cue script also contains the blinding scene, in a hand differing from that for Hermione's cue-script. A version of *King John* (4.1.1–133 in a modern text) labeled "Dick's part" may refer to the actor who played Hubert.

16 For an expansive account of this anecdote, see Alan Hughes, *Henry Irving, Shakespearean* (Cambridge: Cambridge University Press, 1981), 174.

17 Production costs for Irving's Lyceum production exceeded £2,000; *Merchant* ran uninterrupted for 250 performances. See Roger Manvell, *Ellen Terry* (New York: G.P. Putnam, 1968), 128.

18 Bingham, *"The Great Lover":The Life and Art of Herbert Beerbohm Tree* (London: Hamish Hamilton, 1978), 167. St. John cited in Manvell, *Ellen Terry*.

19 The British Library shelfmark reads SC7 H1 Printed ed. of *Merchant of Venice*, with cuts and notes by ET—BL Loan MS 125/42.

20 See Michel de Certeau, "Reading as Poaching," *The Practice of Everyday Life*, trans. Steven Rendell [1984] (University of California Press, 1988), esp. 173.

21 See *Shakespeare's Play of The Merchant of Venice, Arranged for Representation at the Princess's Theatre, with Historical and Explanatory Notes by Charles Kean, as First Performed on Saturday, June 12, 1858* (London: John K. Chapman and Co., 1858), viii, 85, 2.

22 Act, scene and line references are from *The Merchant of Venice*, ed. John Russell Brown; Arden 2 (London: Methuen, 1955; rpt. 1969).

23 See note 10 above and Manvell, *Ellen Terry*, 346.

24 A discrepancy exists between the published cast list—nineteen names, including Morocco—and those roles the script mentions: Portia, Nerissa, Bassanio, Antonio, Gratiano, Balthazar, Solanio, Shylock, Tubal, the Duke.

25 Squire Bancroft and Marie Bancroft, "Four Failures," in *The Bancrofts: Recollections of Sixty Years . . . with Portraits and Illustrations* (New York: E.P. Dutton and Co., 1909), 191–213. "Failures" refers to financial failures.

26 See Edward W. Godwin, F.S.A. "The Architecture and Costume of *The Merchant of Venice*," *The Mask*, ed. Edward Gordon Craig, 1–3 (1908–1911), 75–82. Although Bancroft did not formally acknowledge Godwin, his proposed layouts of stage space may well have offered models for performance.

27 Terry cited in Manvell, *Ellen Terry*, 88–89.

28 Bancroft, "Our Joint Narrative," in *The Bancrofts*, 22.

29 Bancroft, "Season of 1874–75," in *The Bancrofts*, 17.

30 Bancroft, "Our Joint Narrative," 16–17.

31 In a modern text, the lines derive selectively from 2.7.5; 2.9.925–926; 2.9.9–20.

32 See Alice Comyns-Carr, *J. Comyns Carr; Stray Memories, by His Wife* (London: Macmillan and Co., 1920), 30. She remarks: "Neither the fashion of the dress or the coiffure were perhaps as correct to the period as the costumes which I designed for her later on for the better remembered run of *The Merchant of Venice* at the Lyceum."

33 Terry, *The Story of My Life: Recollections and Reflections* (New York: McClure Co., 1908), 46.

34 See Terry, *Memoirs* (New York: Putnam's Sons, 1932), cited in Manvell, *Ellen Terry*, 89; Michael Booth, "Pictorial Acting and Ellen Terry," in *Shakespeare and the Victorian Stage*, ed. Richard Foulkes (Cambridge: Cambridge University Press, 1986), 86; and Nina Auerbach, who remarks that Terry "enticed audiences to look less at her than beyond her to a realm where even forbidden roles could be played"—see "Introduction: Ellen Terry's Lost Lives," in *Ellen Terry: Spheres of Influence*, ed. Katherine Cockin (London: Pickering and Chatto, 2011), 13–16. See also Godwin, "Architecture and Costume of Shakespeare's Plays," 196–197 and "A Lecture on Dress," *The Mask* 6.4 (1914), 335–352.

35 See Laura Mulvey, "Visual Pleasure and Narrative Cinema," in Mulvey, *Visual and Other Pleasures* (Bloomington, IN: Indiana University Press, 1989). (Originally in *Screen* 16.3 (Autumn 1975), 6–18.)

36 See "At the Prince of Wales's," *Punch* (1 May 1875), 186.

37 See Robertson, 1931, 54–55 cited in Booth, "Pictorial Acting," 86.

38 See Fanny Baldwin, "E.W. Godwin and Design for the Theater," in *E.W. Godwin: Aesthetic Movement Architect and Designer*, ed. Susan Weber Soros (New Haven, CT: Yale University Press, 1999), 317–319.

39 The program credits Meredith Bell for the music. First Folio as well as nineteenth-century texts include a song at this point (3.2.63–72 in a modern text). See Laurie

Maguire, *Shakespearean Suspect Texts: The "Bad" Quartos and Their Contexts* (Cambridge: Cambridge University Press, 1996).

40 Terry speaks of being in the habit of directing herself as well as others—see Terry, *Four Lectures on Shakespeare*, ed. and with an introduction by Christopher St John (London: Hopkinson, 1932), 117; see also Alan Hughes, *Henry Irving, Shakespearean*, 16. By the time she was working with Irving, Terry often helped to direct the women in the cast.

41 According to Comyns-Carr, Portia appears in black robes rather than in the scarlet gown worn by her predecessors and mentioned in stage histories. See, for example, *The Merchant of Venice*, ed. John Russell Brown, Arden 2 edition (London: Methuen & Co., 1969); also Alice Vansittart Comyns-Carr, *J. Comyns-Carr: Stray Memories, By His Wife* (London: Macmillan and Co., 1920).

42 See Godwin, "Architecture," 79.

43 My thanks to Richard Abel for the connection to "punch"; on kinesthesia, see Susan Leigh Foster, *Choreographing Empathy: Kinesthesia in Performance* (London and New York: Routledge, 2011).

44 Dr. Valpy may be Richard Valpy, a schoolmaster; one of his claims to notoriety is that he bowdlerized *Henry IV* by removing "some tedious parts." DNB (*Dictionary of National Biography*).

45 Terry, *The Story of My Life*, 115.

46 McKellen's rehearsal script is at the V&A Theatre and Performance Archive. Pages are numbered 3–111; those pages missing are 4, 52, 107–110. The text conflates Quarto and Folio, as in the Arden 2 edition, R.A. Foakes, ed. (Walton-on-Thames: Thomas Nelson and Sons, 1997). The disappearance and reappearance of the writing evokes Freud's mystic writing pad—see "Notes on the Mystic Writing Pad," trans. James Strachey et al., in *The Standard Edition of the Complete Psychological Works of Sigmund Freud*, vol. 19, ed. James Strachey (London: Hogarth Press and Institute of Psycho-Analysis, 1961), 229–230.

47 On restoring erased or layered texts—materials that otherwise would remain invisible—see Reviel Netz and William Noel, *The Archimedes Codex: How a Medieval Prayer Brook Is Revealing the True Genius of Antiquity's Greatest Scientist* (London: Weidenfeld & Nicholson, 2007). Despite help from the National Reconnaissance Office, part of the US government's intelligence community, some markings resist visibility. According to Blythe House archivists, finding erasures on actors' scripts and promptcopies is not unusual; they even see evidence of people using liquid paper or pasting paper slips over original documents.

48 I paraphrase Carolyn Steedman, *Dust: The Archive and Cultural History* (New Brunswick, NJ: Rutgers University Press, 2002), 143–144. See also Louis Mink, "Everyman His Other Analyst," *Critical Inquiry* 7.4 (1981), 777–783. On anecdotes as theory, see Gay McAuley, *Not Magic But Work: An Ethnographic Account of a Rehearsal Process* (Manchester: Manchester University Press, 2012), esp. 155–156.

49 See *Roma al tempo di Giulio III; la pianta di Roma di Leonardo Bufalini del 1551*. Franz Ehrle, Biblioteca apostolica vaticana (Rome: Danese, 1911).

50 See Lahr, "He That Plays the King," *The New Yorker* v. 83.25 (27 August 2007), 53–54.

51 Lahr, "Plays the King," 53.

52 See Roland Barthes, "The Grain of the Voice," in *Image/Music/Text*, trans. Stephen Heath (New York: Hill and Wang, 1977), 179–189. See also Konstantin Stanislavski, *An Actor's Work on a Role*, trans. and ed. Jean Benedetti (London and New York: Routledge, 2010).

53 I borrow the phrase from Netz and Noel, *Archimedes Codex*, 211.

54 McKellen quoted in Lahr, "Plays the King," 50.

55 Walter's script is an 8½ × 11 letter size bound copy; its cover reads DONMAR in large block letters on a black strip down its left edge; Walter's name ("Harriet") is in her hand.

56 See David Daniell, ed. *Julius Caesar*, Arden 3 edition (London: Thomas Nelson and Sons, 1998).

57 See Jonathan Gil Harris, *Untimely Matter in the Time of Shakespeare* (Philadelphia, PA: University of Pennsylvania Press, 2009), esp. 19–20; see also Jeffrey Todd Knight, "Making Shakespeare's Books: Assembly and Intertextuality in the Archives," *Shakespeare Quarterly* 60.3 (2009), 304–340.

58 See Arden 3 edition, 1.3.96–103.

59 See Foster, *Choreographing Empathy*. See also Kemp, *Embodied Acting*, 13.

60 Phillida Lloyd, the director, suggests several readings: *Classics for Dummies*, Allan Massie's *The Caesars*, Kate Gilliver's *Caesar's Gallic Wars*.

61 I borrow this phrase from John Berger's title.

62 See Joseph Kickasola, "Decalogue V and a Short Film about Killing," in Kickasola, *The Films of Krzysztof Kieslowski: The Liminal Image* (New York: Continuum, 2004), 200–210. See also Patrick Colm Hogan, "Tragic Lives: On the Incompatibility of Law and Ethics," *College English* 35.3 (Summer 2008), esp. 16–19; Paul Coates, ed. *Lucid Dreams: The Films of Krzysztof Kieslowski* (Wiltshire, UK: Flicks Books, 1999); and Antonio R. Damasio, *The Feeling of What Happens: Body and Emotion in the Making of Consciousness* (New York and London: Harcourt Brace & Company, 1999), esp. 79–80.

63 Kaos Cinematografica production in collaboration with RAI Cinema, 76 minutes; the film won the Golden Bear award at the Berlin film Festival, February 2012.

64 Manohla Dargis, *New York Times* (5 February 2013). http://nytimes.com/2013/02/06movies/caesar-must-die, accessed March 11, 2014. See also Maurizio Calbi, "'In States Unborn and Accents Yet Unknown': Spectral Shakespeare in Paolo and Vittorio Taviani's *Cesare deve morire* (*Caesar Must Die*)," *Shakespeare Bulletin* 32.2 (2014), 235–253; and Niels Herold, "Movers and Losers: Shakespeare in Charge and Shakespeare Behind Bars," in *Native Shakespeares: Indigenous Appropriations on a Global Stage*, ed. Craig Dionne and Parmita Kapadia (London: Ashgate, 2008), 153–169.

65 Beckett was greatly interested in performances of his plays that took place in prisons. The 1953 Luttringhausen Prison (near Wuppertal in Germany) and the 1957 San Quentin Prison's productions of *Waiting for Godot* were the subject of Jacob Adams' documentary film, *The Impossible Itself* (2010).

66 See Susan Leigh Foster, "An Introduction to Moving Bodies," in Foster, ed., *Choreographing History* (Bloomington, IN: Indiana University Press, 1995), 7, 9, 15.

67 Actioning derives from Stanislavski's work at the Moscow Arts Theatre and is perhaps one of the closest mergers of Russian, British and American acting practices. See Stanislavski, *An Actor's Work on a Role*, trans. and ed. Jean Benedetti (London and New York: Routledge, 2010).

68 Stanislavski posits a through-line that *begins* before the play begins and ends *after* the final curtain. "Real acting begins," Stanislavski remarks, "when there is not character as yet, but an 'I' in the hypothetical circumstances"—see Vasili Toporkov, *Stanislavski in Rehearsal*, trans. and intro. Jean Benedetti (London: Methuen, 2001), 110.

69 See Foster, *Choreographing Empathy*, 9, 13–15. On the linguistic materiality of the body, see also Andre Lepecki, *Exhausting Dance: Performance and the Politics of Movement* (London and New York: Routledge, 2006).

70 For a definition of verbal overshadowing as a strategy aimed at confining the performer and inhibiting imagination, see *Scientific Approaches to Consciousness*, ed. Jonathan D. Cohen and Jonathan W. Schooler. Carnegie Mellon Symposia on Cognition (Mahwah, NJ: L. Erlbaum Associates, 1997), 130. See also Damasio, *Feeling*.

71 See Fischer-Lichte, "Appearing as Embodied Mind: Defining a Weak, a Strong and a Radical Concept of Presence," in *Archaeologies of Presence*, ed. Gabriella Giannachi et al. (London and New York: Routledge, 2012), esp. 114–116; and Rick Kemp, *Embodied Acting: What Neuroscience Tells Us About Performance* (London and New York: Routledge, 2012), 93.

72 Fischer-Lichte, "Appearing," 106.

73 See, for example, Gardner Mack, "Expert Bewails Tendency to Star 'Punch' Instead of the Story," *The Washington Times* (May 29, 1915), 15.

74 See Rebecca Schneider, *Performance Remains: Art and War in Times of Theatrical Reenactment* (London and New York: Routledge, 2011), esp. 13–14. Brutus' repetition of Cassius' comment—"How many times shall Caesar bleed in sport/That now lies fallen on the senate floor/No worthier than the dust"—is underlined but also crossed through.

75 I borrow from Farge, *Allure*, 11.

76 For example, in *The Year of the King: An Actor's Diary and Sketchbook* (London: Chatto and Windus, 1985) and *Beside Myself: An Autobiography* (London: Hutchinson, 2001).

77 Jerome J. McGann, *The Textual Condition* (Princton, NJ: Princeton University Press, 1991).

78 *Beside Myself*, 106. Sher's drawings have appeared in exhibitions at London's National Theatre and in Antony Sher, *Characters, Paintings, Drawings, Sketches* (London: Nick Hern Books, 1989).

79 Berger, *Bento's Sketchbook* (New York: Pantheon Books, 2011), esp. 72, 150, 156, 249. See also Damasio, *Feeling*.

80 I paraphrase Berger, *Bento's Sketchbook*, 72. See also Derrida, *The Postcard: From Socrates to Freud and Beyond*, trans. Alan Bass (Chicago, IL and London: Chicago University Press, 1987), 208–210.

81 See Richard deCordova, *Picture Personalities: The Emergence of the Star System in America* (Champaign, IL: University of Illinois Press, 1990), 19–20. See also William H. Sherman, *Used Books: Marking Readers in Renaissance England* (Philadelphia, PA: University of Pennsylvania Press, 2008), esp. 127, 123.

82 States, *Great Reckonings in Little Rooms: On the Phenomenology of Theater* (Berkeley, CA: University of California Press, 1985), 125.

83 See *Walter Benjamin's Archive*, ed. Ursula Marx et al., trans Esther Lewis (London and New York: Verso, 2007, 73); and Berger, *Bento's Sketchbook*, 9. Derrida writes, "The unconscious text is already a weave of pure traces, differences in which meaning and force are united—a text nowhere present, consisting of archives which are always already transcriptions."—See "Freud and the Scene of Writing," in *Writing and Difference*, trans. Alan Bass (Chicago, IL: Chicago University Press, 1978), 211.

84 I borrow the idea of a theatre of encounter from Asynith Palmer.

85 Benjamin, *The Arcades Project*, trans. Howard Eiland and Kevin McLaughlin (Cambridge, MA: Harvard University Press, 1999), 463.

86 See Lawrence Lipking, "The Marginal Gloss," *Critical Inquiry* 3.4 (Summer 1977), 610, 640, 646–647, 612.

87 Sher, *Beside Myself*, 166.

88 Bachelard, *The Poetics of Space*, trans. Maria Jolas (Boston, MA: Beacon Press, 1994) and States, *Great Reckonings*, 152–154.

89 Foster, "Choreographies of Gender," *Signs* 24.1 (Autumn 1998), 7–8.

90 In order, notes come from a first-half run-through, a week before first preview and a Barbican dress rehearsal.

91 Sher, *Year of the King*, 150.

92 Sher, *Beside Myself*, 343–344. The image came from a book of Boer War photographs (the Victorians photographed their dead infants); Sher also gave a copy of the photograph to Harriet Walter, his Lady Macbeth.

93 Sher, *Year of the King*, 176–177.

94 See *On the Technique of Acting*, ed. Mel Cordon, 118, released as Michael Chekhov, *On Theatre and the Art of Acting*, Working Arts Library.

95 *Beside Myself*, 266.

96 Sher used National Health Service crutches during rehearsal; Brian McKnight fashioned the one he used in performance, and Roger Howell, the RSC's "unofficial" historian, now owns the crutch. Photograph by Helen Hargest of the Shakespeare Centre Library. See also Alice Rayner, *Ghosts: Death's Double and the Phenomena of Theatre* (Minneapolis, MN: University of Minnesota Press, 2006), 89–90, 92.

97 See Matthew Reason, "Archive or Memory? The Detritus of Live Performance," *New Theatre Quarterly* 19.1 (February 2003), 82–89; and Sherry Turkle, *Evocative Objects: Things to Think With* (Cambridge, MA: MIT Press, 2007), 6.

98 Sher sees Fool as "an early incarnation of Sam Beckett arising in Shakespeare's soul"— *Beside Myself*, 116. See also Berger, *Bento's Sketchbook*, 150, 156.

99 See Sher, "The Fool in *King Lear*," in *Players 2*, ed. Russell Jackson and Robert Smallwood (Cambridge: Cambridge University Press, 1988), 156. See also Freddie Rokem, *Philosophers and Thespians: Thinking Performance* (Redwood City, CA: Stanford University Press, 2010), 172.

100 Preiss, "Robert Armin Do the Police in Different Voices," in *From Performance to Print in Shakespeare's England*, eds. Peter Holland and Stephen Orgel (Houndsmill, Basingstoke: Palgrave Macmillan, 2006).

101 Walter Benjamin, "A Small History of Photography," in Benjamin, *One-Way Street and Other Writings*, trans. Edmund Jephcott and Kingsley Shorter (London: New Left Books, 1979), 242.

3

STORYTELLING, ANECDOTES, ETHNOGRAPHY

The ESC's *Wars of the Roses*

The story I want to tell is the story of a band of brothers, of groups and groupings as they appear in rehearsal photographs of *The Wars of the Roses*. My story could begin with the two times I saw the ESC's *Henries*—1 and *2 Henry IV* and *Henry V*, directed by Michael Bogdanov with the assistance of Michael Pennington—first in Toronto and again in London.[1] What I remember was being immediately caught by the opening when, in working lights, most of the cast, wearing rehearsal clothes, stepped forward, led by the actor who would play Poins (Hal's Horatio), to sing:

> Come all you good people, who would hear a song
> Of men brave and men bold and men weak and men strong,
> Of a king who was mighty but wild as a boy
> And list to the ballad of Harry le Roy.

Just as there are several (familiar) stories lurking here, there are several genealogies of presence apparent in the sights and sounds documenting *Wars'* Falstaff, initially played by John Woodvine in the ESC's trilogy, *The Henries*. Writes Michael Pennington, "Within John's slim frame is a fat man bursting to come out.... [He] gave the performance of a lifetime."[2] Anecdote as theory: when Paul Thompson, an elderly gentleman and a friend who also attended the ESC's Toronto performance, saw Woodvine enter as *Henry V*'s Chorus, smartly turned out in grey slacks and blue blazer, he gasped. After the performance, he was still stunned: "But that can't be the same actor: his Falstaff was a very fat man." Clearly, in his mind—and mine—the actor, not the king, was the hero of the ESC's local theatrical neighborhood.

Beginnings. *Wars* arose from rehearsal spaces in Army drill halls, at Wandsworth and Clapham, a mirrored space at Pineapple dance studios near Baker Street and a freezing near-derelict warehouse on the Thames Dockland, and from a vast ex-Flying Boat Aircraft hangar off Plymouth Sound, the Regency comfort of the Bath

Theatre Royal and Melbourne's Victoria Institute. In the words of photographer Laurence Burns, *Wars* stormed:

> "To France" or "To the Breach" or slo-mo-ed a choreographed clash of armour and swords to smoke machines and an emotional classical chamber music sound recording, as punk young Henry had his leery way with Doll Tearsheet while Falstaff idled, having his cold toes warmed at Mistress Quickly's seacoal fire—but always headed for his personal curtain call on time![3]

In large part, my story engages with Laurence Burns' photographic account of the ESC's work. He was shooting all the time—from early rehearsals through to the filming of a last performance at the Grand Theatre, Swansea. I think of *Wars* as Theatre-in-Transit, in several senses: literal travel across a broad international range and travel between rehearsal and performance, a flexible arena where slippage occurs between those terms and is conditioned, perhaps even altered, when performed in venues as disparate as Hull and Hong Kong, Toronto and Tokyo, Bath and Berlin, Cardiff and Chicago.[4] Yet although Bogdanov and Pennington apparently gave Burns free rein, their account of *Wars'* making mentions him only in initialed captions for a scattering of published photographs. Those photographs, together with a select number of others, offer empirical traces that track *Wars'* unfolding narrative and grounds my multi-layered account. Previously un-remarked, they merit closer looking.[5]

Performance is haunted by writing,[6] and in two directions: rehearsal notes, dressers' notes, deputy stage manager's promptbook and stage manager's book bring them into being, into embodiment; reviews, criticism, blogs and other social media re-imagine performance with the aid of memory. Both forms of writing constitute indexical signs of the performance event. Whereas John Barton and Peter Hall's *Wars of the Roses* (1964) constitutes a literary collage stitched together with Barton's imitative Shakespearean verse, the ESC's *Wars of the Roses* (1986–1989) is primarily all Shakespeare, all the time, except for two invented paratexts and one "translation" that lead or enhance crucial moments. First is the opening ballad, which details Hal's progress from tavern roustabout to king; second, the Prologue to *Richard III*, spoken by a narrator who introduces everyone, placing them in groups for easier identification in *Wars'* soap-operatic tale; third, the Lady Mortimer scene (*I Henry IV*, 3.1), translating "*The Lady speaks in Welsh*") into Welsh. Burns' photographs, however, move away from language to image: faster than lightning flashes, they chronicle the developing collaboration between director, actors and photographer, figuring voice as image, as visual presence. Not only do photographs constitute the stuff of memory—the way in which the brain internally displays thought to itself—but thinking itself involves scenography, the staging of perceptions into the spectacle of ideas. "Memory," writes Walter Benjamin, "is not an instrument for exploring the past but its theatre."[7] Read phenomenologically, what are the effects and affects of Burns' compositions, of his framing and re-framing, of his artistic manipulations?[8]

Riffing with remains: "room-for-play"

For one thing, these "Speaking Pictures" invite thinking diachronically and thematically, emphasizing the shift from words to images, a transformation that relies on and emphasizes bodies.[9] A "happy disorder," writes Benjamin, who grounds his methodology on literary montage: "I needn't say anything. Merely show."[10] Keeping in mind that photographs do not describe in the same way as writing nor do they share the same temporality as text, this selection gives some idea of the impressive range of Burns' work, fashions an account of *Wars* by riffing on a unique set of remains.[11]

Three photographs. One marks the beginning of *Wars*, the second and third its ending. Each frames Bogdanov differently, though each surrounds him with theatre practitioners, whether actors or technicians. The first (Figure 3.1), shows a blurred background where, holding a wine glass, Bogdanov is encircled by actors (not readily identifiable), the backs of two form a wall, nearly blocking him from view. In the close foreground, wearing a white shirt and light sweater, John Woodvine—who will play Falstaff—sits apart, as if already excluded from the others, listening to music (what does Falstaff listen to—jazz? ballads? easy listening?), reading what I imagine to be an early version of the script for *Wars*—two of his senses muted,

FIGURE 3.1 John Woodvine reading; Michael Bogdanov framed by cast members in background. Photograph © Laurence Burns.

focused inward. The two fields in the shot vie with one another, but Woodvine's presence, in sharp contrast, is the more compelling.[12]

A second photograph (Figure 3.2), taken at the filming in the Grand Theatre, Swansea, shows a cameraman in the left foreground, a centered camera and tripod, with a script pinned to the camera and, in the right background, the scene being shot—Michael Pennington's Hal bending over Michael Cronin's Henry IV, the crown visible on his pillow. The shot is built upon a triangle in a "closed-form" design[13] that highlights both the film-making process and the script of storytelling. The cameraman's look and the camera lens lead the viewer's eye to the shot's defining moment: the triangle's apex, Hal and Henry IV. And the centered camera can be read as a displaced extension of Burns' own still camera. The composition also draws a viewer's attention to the dazzling white page of the script attached to the camera—and contesting its authority—as if to privilege the text orchestrating the scene and the long-absent author.

The third image (Figure 3.3) reverses the angle of the previous photo and rearranges the scene. This is a "stop-motion" shot: everyone in it appears arrested, as in a game of musical chairs, from the figure checking a light meter at left frame to the cameraman behind the camera and tripod and the costumed actor beside the tripod in the right background. Gesturing with his hands as though framing a shot, Bogdanov, the label on his workman's shirt aligning him with *Dream*'s handcraft men, casts an intense look past Cronin, barely visible in the foreground, towards

FIGURE 3.2 Filming Hal (Michael Pennington) and Henry IV (Michael Cronin). "Crown scene" in rehearsal for filming *Wars* at the Grand Swansea Theatre. Centered camera on tripod, script pinned to camera; cameraman in left frame. Photograph © Laurence Burns.

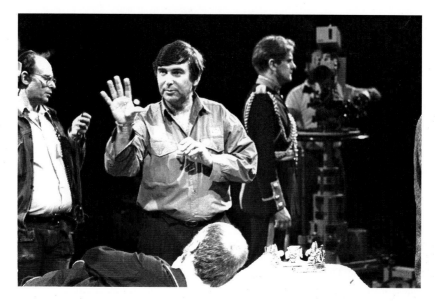

FIGURE 3.3 Michael Bogdanov framing a photograph of the "Crown scene."
Rehearsal for filming *Wars* at the Grand Swansea Theatre. Photograph ©
Laurence Burns.

the spectator—or, rather, at a select spectator, Michael Pennington, probably
standing beside Burns—an absent presence in this moment, when Hal, thinking his
father dead, "steals" the crown. The camera and tripod anchor one side of a
parallelogram or the apex of a triangle, depending on whether one focuses on the
actors' bodies and heads or on Bogdanov's hands (does his gesture seek out
Pennington among the viewers, perhaps invite his approval?). Flipping from the
second image to the third, the centered figure of Bogdanov now seems to replace
the script, as if to re-assign authorship (and authority) to *Wars*' director.

These photographs can be thought of as a portrait-sketch of *Wars*—stills cut out
from a larger time flow, a phenomenon that blurs categories between fictional
narrative and history. As Steedman writes, "History gave a habitation and a name
to all the fragments, traces—all the inchoate stuff—that has ended up in the
archive"—in this case, "stuff" from several archives: Laurence Burns' photographs,
the Victoria and Albert Theatre and Performance collections and Stratford's
Shakespeare Centre Library. What is in my hands, then, resembles photographic
segments from a mini-film script—focusing at times on a series of "one-offs," at
others, on a sequence, generating moments of embodied knowing through Burns'
use of the camera as a choreographic tool.[14]

Beginners

Two photographs constitute a framework for what might be called a performed
ethnography—that is, a series of references to the temporal trajectories of rehearsal

FIGURE 3.4 Company meeting, Territorial Army Headquarters, Wandsworth. English Shakespeare Company's first rehearsal for *Wars of the Roses*. Michael Bogdanov at upstage left. Photograph © Laurence Burns.

and performance—embodied experiences, anecdotes, gossip, especially insofar as these often work to enhance actors' and spectators' experience of a particular moment or scene.[15]

September 1986: the ESC's initial rehearsal at Wandsworth—a shot that reads like a company meeting rather than a rehearsal per se—no scripts are in evidence, for instance—that documents the size of the company. No one is singled out as primary—a glance at the company as a band of brothers; some figures, their backs to the camera, are not clearly identifiable. In addition to Bogdanov and Pennington, twenty-one actors (of a cast of twenty-five) are present; others, partially off-screen, their bodies cut out by the shot's frame, are there only as "body parts." Once, it was customary for the Admiral's Men to meet at the Sun Tavern in Fish Street for a preliminary reading: Henslowe paid for the drinks and recorded the amount—5 shillings—for reimbursement.[16] Might this image capture a similar moment? Drinks may go missing, though most players are laughing—at a story, an anecdote, a joke, or perhaps with pleasure at the audacious project being outlined?

A serious reading of Figure 3.5 depicting Bogdanov kneeling beside a ramp on wheels, setting a miniature staircase beside it, would view him as checking the right angle for the ramp. In a lighter vein, he could be playing with a toy, as if staging a miniature war game or a child's version of *Wars*, suitable for a doll's house. Which might Burns be imagining?

FIGURE 3.5 Michael Bogdanov checking angle of ramp. Rehearsal. Alford House ("Awful House"), Kennington. Photograph © Laurence Burns.

Identities: body-shaping

From this point forward, I alternate between solo moments, points of contact that make and remake the ESC's "world" and sequences that re-inhabit and deconstruct several crisis points, tracing their unfolding from rehearsal to performance.

Burns' photograph of John Price does double duty, giving his extraordinary presence (his jacket read "Hal's Angels") a room of his own and paying homage to his loss. Here, he is lifted from the center of a tavern group and photographed alone, in the darkened space, chairs and tables visible at right frame. He fires one (authentic?) gun into the empty air behind him, its partner ready in his left hand: a solo turn for an especially energetic actor who died in 1987—a stand-in for others lost along the way to Swansea's filming.

John Woodvine as Falstaff, his rehearsal persona anticipating performance. Before turning to this "body double," I want to "half-way" imagine another, a shot that has gone missing: Woodvine in Falstaff's fat suit. I say half-way because such an image does exist, taken by John Tramper, who, like many ESC actors, played a number of roles.[17] Woodvine, his eyes wide open, grins at the camera; his hands lift his shirt, revealing the full extent of his padded fatness; his right hand holds a rather loud paisley tie—ready to adorn his body. Although some sequences showing rehearsal and performance reveal a close "marriage" between the two, primarily effected through a costume change, this one—"Falstaff Unplugged" (his mp3 device stuffed in his pocket)—recalls his initial image (see Figure 3.1), where he also is listening to music. His sly look off right frame—peripheral vision loaded with meaning—tops a body rooted in space; his coffee mug, held delicately in his right hand as though it were made of fine china, becomes transformed, in another shot, into a shining

FIGURE 3.6 John Woodvine holding coffee mug. Rehearsal for filming at Grand Swansea Theatre. Photograph © Laurence Burns.

FIGURE 3.7 Falstaff (John Woodvine) mixing a drink. Performance. Grand Swansea Theatre. Photograph © Laurence Burns.

pewter tankard, ready to be filled with a cocktail of remains and a raw egg—the classic "hair of the dog" hangover cure—all the more potent given the whiskey bottle near at hand. Judging from Falstaff's expression, this is a weighty business.

A hyped-up quartet off to conquer France, coming toward camera, armed for travel in this theatre of expediency with a boom box, a suitcase, a briefcase and a shoulder-hung kit bag. Framed by "towers," black curtains dress the far background space: a center triangular opening reveals a hidden watcher—mirrored by Pennington and Bogdanov, backs to the camera, in the near foreground (I imagine them urging "More! More!"). In answer to that request, several images from a five- to six-shot sequence eventually show a banner reading "Fuck the Frogs" suspended from the balcony level—a "joke" not appreciated in Francophone Canada.[18]

A cluster of objects—ladders, a flatbed cart, a bicycle, a trash can, a shopping cart, a few wooden chairs, a cupboard, tables with hand props, even a few huddled actors—have been pushed against the back wall of the rehearsal space; two overturned tables frame a couch at mid-foreground, a set-up for the first shot. His figure outlined in a shaft of light from windows in the upper background wall, Pennington stands on a small table, urging forward a rag-tag dozen crowded together on the foreground side of the barrier, a few with mock rifles. One hand to his head, perhaps wondering if the scene looks right, Bogdanov watches from the left foreground, monitoring his "army": a (borrowed) title tells it all: "This is a marvelous convenient place for our rehearsal." The second shot in the sequence

FIGURE 3.8 Off to France. Rehearsal, Alford House ("Awful House"), Kennington. Watched by Michael Bogdanov (right frame) and Michael Pennington (left frame), backs to camera. Photograph © Laurence Burns.

FIGURE 3.9 "Once More Unto the Breach." Rehearsal. Michael Bogdanov, hands to head, watching in left-center foreground. Territorial Army Headquarters, Wandsworth. Photograph © Laurence Burns.

FIGURE 3.10 "Once More Unto the Breach." Rehearsal. Territorial Army Headquarters, Wandsworth. Photograph © Laurence Burns.

shows Pennington in profile, an ethereal figure in the streaming light, his own mock rifle raised high, as several men, echoing his gesture, cross the barrier while four still crouch behind it. In the third shot, most players are moving toward the far wall; at right frame, one man supports a wounded comrade and another leans

FIGURE 3.11 "Once More Unto the Breach." Rehearsal. End of Scene. Territorial Army Headquarters, Wandsworth.

FIGURE 3.12 "Once More Unto the Breach." Performance. Grand Swansea Theatre. Photograph © Laurence Burns.

over the couch arm, as if wounded or dead. Pennington, still centered in the group (all in soft focus), also faces the back wall: his stilled figure, having moved past the now-empty table, is not readily distinguishable among the band of brothers. My attention, then, is drawn to the four actors in sharp focus in front of the barrier, two with their heads down, perhaps wounded or hiding in fear.

As Burns constructs "presence"—a mode of work that articulates the intervals and slips of tenses and times in the space and practice of the image itself—he effectively replaces Bogdanov as director, especially in the second and third shots, organizing not just the space but also the act of looking itself. This is particularly evident in the photograph from the Breach sequence in preview. Rehearsal's overturned tables and couch have become sandbags; the soldiers are still costumed in rag-tag outfits, some in tin hats; at left frame, several, one pointing a rifle, have leapt the barrier, encircling one side of it while four remain behind, two with their heads down, wounded or hiding in fear. Henry, astride a slanted tank turret at right frame, his gun held aloft, his elevated figure bathed in swirling light that transforms him into an illusion, a phantom, as he hails these "groundlings" into battle. The triangle formed by the soldier's rifle and Henry's raised arm intensifies the tension, drawing its energy from the brilliantly swirling light. The shaft of light from an upper background window illuminating the scene in rehearsal becomes, in this preview photograph, lit as in a cathedral, turning Henry's figure, poised above his soldiers, into an heroic idol. Burns' manipulation of the image through multiple exposures creates a kind of sensation scene, with the other-worldly spectral figure of Henry a fitting climax to his incantatory speech.

Rejecting Falstaff

A story within a story: a meditation on *Wars'* defining moment: four shots of Falstaff's rejection document how framing and re-framing encodes the photograph, attuning it to space, which not only marks the segue between one instance

FIGURE 3.13 Falstaff's Rejection (1). Territorial Army Headquarters, Wandsworth. Photograph © Laurence Burns.

of rehearsal to the other—theatre-in-transit—but also invites thinking of the broader contexts before and beyond this moment. These images offer a perfect instance of how privileging the physical text over the verbal text, in Augusto Boal's phrase, "makes thought *visible*,"[19] of how serial tableaux take a cue from silent film or its predecessors in an unusually sustained flip book. A viewer puts the still (back) into motion in this performative sequence of shots wherein each shot also is a performance.[20]

Although the actions span two discrete scenes—beadles ousting the tavern group; the events surrounding the rejection itself—the initial shot encompasses both, but acknowledges the textual structure by generating the illusion of an architectural gap between them. That gap points to Pennington's use of Orson Welles' 1966 film, *Chimes at Midnight*, which reverses moments of *Henry IV, Part I*'s final scene to leave Hal still at odds with his father—the King believing that Falstaff has indeed killed Hotspur and that Hal's claim to do so is a lie.[21] The arrest of the tavern crew (here, two women) occupies the near foreground, the violence of that action distinctly opposed to the royal party, a line of offstage actors posed against the upper background wall, intent on the scene before them; only Pennington's Henry is "on," his body already has assumed the rigid pose that he will wear like a mask from this point forward. His hands are at his sides, as though holding onto himself, cutting himself apart from others; a primly proper woman in white stands at his left, a striking contrast to the unruly women in the foreground.

In the segue to the next shot (I'm imagining a time gap; no actors occupy the background now, though the bicycle—whose? Used for what?—a ladder, trashcan and prop table remain), Falstaff enters at right frame. What does he see? He's looking at the King—may a Falstaff look at a king?—or, more precisely, looking at Hal "in" King Henry V.[22] Woodvine's whole body registers joyful anticipation (all-eager-all-over, like a child at a birthday party), one foot lifted, as though on tiptoe, his arms half-ready for an embrace. Pennington, eyes fixed front, strides slowly, formally down an aisle formed between two lines of four ranked brothers and courtiers that read as one, their eyes slightly cast down, not looking at Henry or Falstaff. This is a story of doubled presences.

Hal-Henry—the Lord Chief Justice at his side, at the head of one of the columns of actors, now facing front in a military "at ease" position, hands behind their backs—stands at left frame, off center, snarling towards center right at a kneeling Falstaff, his double (or alter ego). His back to the camera, Falstaff's facial expression is unreadable; in terms of scenographic space, he occupies the position between ranked columns of courtiers that Henry has just vacated. Like several of Burns' photographs, this one is a triangular composition of heads and bodies. What is consistently striking is how body language expresses emotional distinctions: Hal's rigid posture on the one hand; Falstaff's submissive entreaty on the other—this might be a sequence from a silent film. The third shot captures seven actors as they march diagonally towards left frame, following after Hal-Henry, who is out of shot. And Falstaff? Uncannily, his gaze is prompted by Hal's absent presence, which leads the eye back to this photograph's defining moment of consequence. Falstaff's right

FIGURE 3.14 Falstaff's Rejection (2). John Woodvine as Falstaff in rehearsal. Territorial Army Headquarters, Wandsworth. Photograph © Laurence Burns.

FIGURE 3.15 Falstaff's Rejection (3). John Woodvine as Falstaff in rehearsal. Territorial Army Headquarters, Wandsworth. Photograph © Laurence Burns.

hand is barely extended, his left held close to his body, his upper body leaning slightly forward, his face stricken with disbelief. Among those who follow Hal-Henry, his figure is the most alert. How does the image read? As a token of the King's power, even when he is absent.

Next, a shift in Falstaff-players, from Woodvine to Barry Stanton, and a shift in rehearsal space to an expansive, high-ceilinged room. Stanton holds a small Union Jack on a stick, so do two actors on a second level atop a gantry on wheels at right frame. Bogdanov's head and shoulders are in the foreground, slightly off-center, generating the illusion that he is closer to the action: the Deputy Stage Manager or Stage Manager, almost cut out of the shot at lower right, is at his side. Pennington wears a horizontally striped pullover and a knotted scarf around his neck; Stanton, bearded, sports a brimmed hat with a Union Jack design, a workman's jacket, shirt and jeans and, like Henry-Hal, a knotted scarf around his neck. Only Pennington and Stanton are captured in movement; other actors stand fixed, part of the scenery, audience for the face-off between the two. Hal-Henry bends forward stiffly at the waist, distancing himself, but the shot's emotional charge again comes from his snarling look, simultaneously threatening and querying the kneeling Falstaff.

Thinking ahead, it would be convenient simply to say that all the actors needed to do was hang their rehearsal clothes on a peg and put on clothing appropriate to their station, chosen from a closetful of paper-doll pret-a-porter costumes, to be read as performance. In one sense, that's absolutely "true": they are surrogates of themselves; clothes *do* make the man—or his effigy. Yet the energies that pulse through the layers of information in rehearsal shots, the richly textured sense of

FIGURE 3.16 Falstaff's Rejection (4). Barry Stanton as Falstaff in rehearsal. Territorial Army Headquarters, Wandsworth. Photograph © Laurence Burns.

presence, of "being there," seem muted.[23] More specifically, what goes missing, perhaps because of the repeated positions and gestures in this shot, is a certain immediacy, a sense of risk: at this way station to performance the shots are on the way to becoming a kind of scenery—one step away from being further arrested: consigned to the archive.

Here, the familiar black backdrop curtain is slightly more open; no one is on the scaffolding; several out-of-focus actors are half-assembled in a column; another group of three at left frame engages in a hurried confab; Falstaff and another actor occupy the foreground. It is tempting to read the shot as text-tied, capturing Falstaff reassuring Justice Shallow that he will pay what is owed him. Yet there's something curiously ambiguous that troubles that context, invites reading it as a rest in rehearsal: any further context is absent, out of shot. Read either way, the photograph—caught on the fly, in process—echoes Falstaff's liminal circumstances.

Kissing cousins

These images of King Henry wooing Princess Katherine invite attention to the actors' movements within the frame—in Susan Leigh Foster's words, reading the

FIGURE 3.17 Henry V (Michael Pennington) and Princess Katherine (Jenny Quayle): Kiss. Performance. Still from filming at Grand Swansea Theatre. 1986. Photograph © Laurence Burns.

FIGURE 3.18 Henry V (Michael Pennington) and Princess Katherine (Jenny Quayle): After the kiss. Performance. Still from filming at Grand Swansea Theatre. 1986. Photograph © Laurence Burns.

"texture and timing of their bodies in motion."[24] As with Richard III wooing Lady Anne, the scene relies on established codes of conduct between gendered bodies, especially, in these shots, who is passive and who active, who is looked at, and who is looking.[25] A black curtain forms a background; the first shot also shows a white scrim patterned with fleur-de-lys, economically locating the scene in France. Setting details as well as costuming—dark versus light—marks their difference; that distinction enhances the tension between the two. Although Henry is in the dominant, right-frame position, his gaze positions Katherine as an object on view, she who is to be looked-at. Her hair formally pinned up, she wears mourning (for France, for kinsmen killed at Agincourt?). Her high-collared gown sheaths her entire body, calling attention to her pale face; in contrast, Henry is in military dress uniform but does not wear a crown. He reaches across her body to grasp her right shoulder, attempting to bring her closer, hold her in place; rigid, eyes downcast, passively resistant, she leans away, barely accepting Henry's kiss. Following the kiss, the two remain close, but their faces, turned in opposite directions, trouble any sense that they are close. Henry's eyes are closed (in apprehension or bliss?); turned away, Katherine's are half open—this image, even more than the other, seems to be "about" *not* looking. Just as these shots of their encounter document stages in a performance, a viewer selects, interprets and becomes imbricated "in" these photographs—participating in the performance by imaginatively refashioning it, as though physical and emotional experiences fuse in "kinesthetic empathy."[26]

Fight cues

Like most theatrical documents, what Bradley calls "Edward Alleyn's scroll" seems to withhold information, merely reading "pugnant" to introduce the duels in *Orlando Furioso* rather than the more elaborate directions and/or marginalia typical of the quarto text—"He fighteth first with one and then with another, and ouercomes them both" and "They fight a good while and then breath"—and of later rehearsal scripts.[27]

Moving to present-day inscriptions, I want to follow the traces of the Shakespearean fight through several modalities. In the text, a combat or duel most commonly is marked simply by "*They fight*"; here, however, "*The Prince killeth Hotspur*" makes that much more precise. David Scott Kastan, a recent editor, conjectures that such precision derives from historical confusion over who killed Hotspur and is intended to mark that in favor of England rather than Scotland.[28] Another trace, recalling *Orlando*, relies on words that provide minimal cues to sequences of action, as in the following excerpt from fight director Malcolm Ranson's annotations for this crucial climactic moment, identifying the separate moves in time that make it up: quoting from two pages in a longer sequence, "Ha cuts down at Ho head; Ho envelopes [*sic*] and cuts Ha R leg; Ha parries; Ho carries on round and cuts Ha L cheek; Ha ducks and cuts across Ho belly; Ho does reverse parry; Ha cuts Ho right leg."[29] Another example, the Richard–Richmond fight, develops its own coded cues. "R drops helm + elbows R1 in the stomach + B/H in the face, turns R1 arm + drops on it, takes hold of the hand + pulls R1 on back. Hits R1 in front of elbow bringing dagg. towards R1 face; R1 brings dagger U/S, Rips off helm; R cuts throat at front; R1 tries to crawl D/S; R cut back of R neck; THE BITTER END." Here, R1 stands for Richard, R for Richmond, though speech prefixes occasionally confuse the two—a "mistake" that seems especially apt. And as in descriptions of McKellen's antic death throes,[30] there is something about the Richard–Richmond fight that prompts deputy stage managers to comment on Richard's death, whether by drawing a stick figure, captioned "DA DA DA DA" or, as here, writing "THE BITTER END." However incomplete, it is possible, given these shots, to intuit how these words generate a sense of moving bodies put into "fast-speed replay"—requiring from performers, as with any risky stage maneuver, a heightened attention to memory.

Burns' photographs constitute yet another mode—occurring halfway between rehearsal and performance, possibly at a preview. Within a minimalist set of mottled grey floor and flat black background wall, both Hal and Hotspur are in costume, as are two watchers in the left background. Hotspur (Andrew Jarvis) wears a kilt and is shirtless, his shaved head encircled with a black band; Hal (Pennington) is in light

FIGURE 3.19 Hal (Michael Pennington) and Hotspur (Anthony Jarvis), multiple exposures of fight (1). Two spectators watch at up-left frame. Late rehearsal. Grand Swansea Theatre. Photograph © Laurence Burns.

FIGURE 3.20 Hal (Michael Pennington) and Hotspur (Anthony Jarvis), multiple exposures of fight (2). Two spectators at up-left frame. Late rehearsal. Grand Swansea Theatre. Photograph © Laurence Burns.

chain mail and a loose tabard. Their multiplying figures resonate with *1 Henry IV* 5.3, where Sir Walter Blunt and others, wearing the King's colors, create the illusion that the King has multiple bodies.[31] Once again setting up a conversation between photography, choreography and the body's time, Burns organizes the space of the shot as well as the act of looking by accentuating the intensity of the action, turning the fight into a multiple-exposure ballet. Instead of a sequence of shots that work to disarticulate a complex action (as in the rejection), these performative set pieces become a kind of "motion exercise," their overall moves "magically" transformed into a horizontal smoke-like blur.[32]

The first photograph creates the vision of two pairs of fighters. In center frame, Hal and Hotspur seem in close combat, but actually Hal is facing off against a second Hotspur prominent in the right foreground, while the first Hotspur confronts a second lunging Hal at left frame: Burns' multiple exposures intensify the sense that neither figure is set firmly on the floor and instead floats or glides above it. In the second shot, Burns again uses multiple exposures to sculpt time, compressing a series of moves into the extravagant dynamism of a single frame. Now three Hotspurs confront at least four Hals, and the former stand out more boldly against the dark background, reversing the textual sense of the latter's dominance. An abstract palimpsest of choreographed bodies and light flashes, the fighters' lower bodies seem insubstantial, their weapons disembodied, one reminiscent of Macbeth's airborne dagger. Superimposed, these multiple bodies appear to circle one another as though the action is about to take flight, creating out of the exhausting fight a phantom-like carousel of play.

FIGURE 3.21 *Wars* cast at curtain call, wearing red noses. Photograph © Laurence Burns, at the Victoria and Albert Theatre and Performance Archive.

FIGURE 3.22 Michael Bogdanov taking curtain call, Grand Swansea Theatre. Cameraman at left frame, focusing camera on audience. Photograph © Laurence Burns.

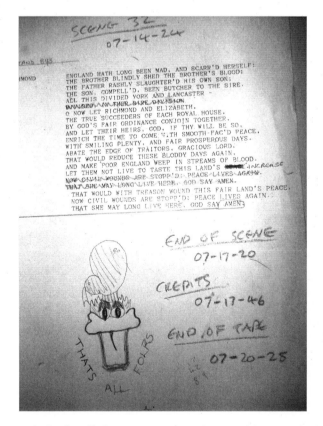

FIGURE 3.23 "That's All, Folks." Promptscript, ESC's *Wars of the Roses*, final page. Photograph © Richard Abel.

Remaining remains

As a finale to this photographic history, consider the cluster of shots above (Figures 3.21–3.23) beginning with the cast and crew at a curtain call: some wear rehearsal clothes, some are in costume, all face off left—a loose grouping resembling the opening, in which actors join in singing *Wars'* opening ballad—a call to listen to history:"Come all you good people, who would hear a song/Of men bold and men brave and men weak and men strong." And all wear Red Noses—the ESC's band of brothers revealed as a cluster of clowns. Of a sudden, Bogdanov—his tiny figure in a doll-house-like empty space, empty except for a scarcely visible cameraman at far left, his camera, now distant, detached from Bogdanov, aimed at an off-frame audience—bows toward that same audience from the stage of the Grand Swansea Theatre, its floor brimming with eponymous red and white roses. In so framing this "stop-motion" shot with his camera, Burns seems to usurp authority from Bogdanov one last time. Yet it is the stage manager, entering from the wings, a comic writer-performer whose "End of Scene, Credits, End of Tape" (in red) trumps and over-trumps them both, sounding the last call, taking his own final bow with a sketch of Daffy Duck from Warner's cartoons, wearing "That's All Folks" like a necklace—a mock heroic epitaph to an epic enterprise.

Notes

1 Ed Mirvish and his son David were in charge of both London's Old Vic, where *The Henries* played from May 18–June 27, 1987, and at Toronto's Royal Alexandra Theatre (March 16–May 2, 1987), where the trilogy turned out to be a mismatch with the Royal Alex's conservative subscription audience: see Ric Knowles, *Reading the Material Theatre* (Cambridge: Cambridge University Press, 2004). The full *Wars of the Roses* included *Richard II, Henry VI, House of Lancaster, Henry VI, House of York* and *Richard III.*

2 Michael Bogdanov and Michael Pennington, *The English Shakespeare Company: The Story of "the Wars of the Roses," 1986–1989* (London: Nick Hern Books, 1990), 20.

3 Laurence Burns email (December 2, 2014).

4 See also Knowles, *Reading the Material Theatre.* "Materialist semiotics" is his term for taking into account all that pertains to meaning in contemporary English-language theatre; he views theory and practice as mutually constitutive.

5 Like Peggy Phelan, I view performance as potentially open to what lies outside the text and is thus "unmarked"—see *Unmarked: The Politics of Performance* (London and New York: Routledge, 1993).

6 See Alice Rayner, *Ghosts: Death's Double and the Phenomena of Theatre* (Minneapolis, MN: University of Minnesota Press, 2006), 55–56.

7 See my "Photography, Theatre, Mnemonics; or, Thirteen Ways of Looking at a Still," in *Theorizing Practice: Redefining Theatre History*, ed. W.B. Worthen and Peter Holland (Basingstoke and New York: Palgrave Macmillan, 2003), 89–90. For the Benjamin quote, see Barbara Maria Stafford, *Visual Analogy: Consciousness as the Art of Connecting* (Cambridge, MA: MIT Press, 1999), 73.

8 See Roland Barthes, *Camera Lucida: Reflections on Photography*, trans. Richard Howard (New York: Hill and Wang, 1981), 20–21.

9 This section is indebted to conversations with Richard Abel.

10 See Walter Benjamin, *The Arcades Project*, trans. Howard Eiland and Kevin McLaughlin (Cambridge, MA: Harvard University Press, 1999), 460 [N1a, 8]; and "Unpacking My Library: A Talk About Book Collecting," in *Selected Writings* vol. 2, Part 2, 1931–1934,

trans. Rodney Livingston and Others, eds. Michael W. Jennings, Howard Eiland, and Gary Smith (Cambridge, MA and London: The Belknap Press of Harvard University Press, 1999), 486–493.

11 See Mike Pearson and Michael Shanks, *Theatre/Archaeology* (London: Routledge, 2001), 43. See also Walter Benjamin, "Excavation and Memory," in *Selected Writings*, Volume 2.2, 1931–1934, ed. Michael W. Jennings et al. (Cambridge, MA: Belknap Press of Harvard University Press, 1999), 576.

12 Woodvine's presence also dates the photograph to 1986–1987; by late 1987 and all performances thereafter, including those within the UK and on the international tour, Barry Stanton played Falstaff.

13 See Terry and Deborah Bolton, *Before the Movies* (New Barnet, UK: John Libby Publishing, 2014; Bloomington, IN: Indiana University Press, 2014), 57.

14 See Carolyn Steedman, *Dust: The Archive and Cultural History* (New Brunswick, NJ: Rutgers University Press, 2002), 67, 149; see also Susan Leigh Foster, *Choreographing Empathy: Kinesthesia in Performance* (London and New York: Routledge, 2011), esp. 4–13. This section also draws *passim* on essays in *Archaeologies of Presence: Art, Performance and the Persistence of Being*, ed. Gabriella Giannachi, Nick Kaye and Michael Shanks (London and New York: Routledge, 2012).

15 See Gay McAuley, *Not Magic But Work: An Ethnographic Account of a Rehearsal Process* (Manchester: Manchester University Press, 2012), esp. 155–156. See also Joseph Roach, *Cities of the Dead: Circum-Atlantic Performance* (New York: Columbia University Press, 1996), 30–33.

16 See David Bradley, *From Text to Performance in the Elizabethan Theatre: Preparing the Play for the Stage* (Cambridge: Cambridge University Press, 1992), 90. See also W.W. Greg, *Two Elizabethan Stage Abridgements: The Battle of Alcazar & Orlando Furioso: An Essay in Critical Bibliography* (Oxford: Clarendon Press, 1923), 135–141.

17 Tramper's photograph of Woodvine appears in Bogdanov and Pennington, *ESC Wars*, facing 67.

18 See Knowles, *Reading the Material Theatre*, esp. 166–169.

19 See Augusto Boal, *Theatre of the Oppressed*, trans. C.A. and M.L. McBride (New York: Theatre Communications Group, 1985), 137; emphasis in original. See also "Boal, Blau, Brecht: The Body" in Phillip Auslander, *From Acting to Performance: Essays in Modernism and Postmodernism* (London and New York, Routledge, 1997), 105.

20 See D.E. Wittkower, *A Preliminary Phenomenology of the Audio Book* (London and New York: Routledge, 2011), 218–225. See also Matthew Rubery, ed., *Audiobooks, Literature and Sound Studies* (London: Routledge, 2011).

21 See Bogdanov and Pennington, *ESC Wars*, 54–55; see also Bridget Gellert Lyons, ed., *Chimes at Midnight: Orson Welles, Director*, Rutgers Films in Print (New Brunswick, NJ: Rutgers University Press, 1988), 178–186.

22 *King Henry IV, Part 2*, ed. A.R. Humphreys (London: Methuen and Co., 1977), 5.4, 5.5. See Barthes, *Camera Lucida*, 3.

23 I draw from Tim Etchells, Gabriella Giannachi and Nick Kaye, "Looking Back: a Conversation about Presence, 2006," in Giannachi et al., *Archaeologies of Presence*, 192.

24 Susan Leigh Foster, "An Introduction to Moving Bodies," in her *Choreographing History* (Bloomington, IN: Indiana University Press, 1995), 9.

25 Susan Leigh Foster, "Choreographies of Gender," *Signs: Journal of Women in Culture and Society* 24.1 (Autumn 1998), 7–8.

26 See Foster, *Choreographing Empathy*, 13–14. See also Deidre Sklar, "Can Bodylore Be Brought to Its Senses?," *Journal of American Folklore* 107.423 (1994), 14, and Jacques Ranciere, *The Emancipated Spectator*, trans. Gregory Elliott (London and New York: Verso, 2009), 13.

27 Bradley, *From Text to Performance*, 25.

28 Kastan, *King Henry IV, Part 1*, Arden 3 edition (London: Thomson Learning, 2002). 5.4.73, 78.

29 Fight sequence from ESC papers held at the Victoria and Albert Theatre and Performance Archive.

30 See Chapter 1, "Material Remains at Play."

31 See David Scott Kastan, ed. *King Henry IV, Part 1*, 5.3.1–27; see also Raphael Holinshed, *The Chronicles of England, Scotland, and Ireland*, 3 vol., 2nd edition (1587), 3.523: Holinshed reports that Douglas "slue Sir Walter Blount, and three other, apparreled in the kings sute and clothing, saieng: 'I marvell to see so many kings thus suddenlie arise one in the necke of an other'."

32 See, for example, late nineteenth-century motion studies of Etienne-Jules Marey, among others: *Lettres d'Etienne-Jules Marey à Georges Demeny 1880–1894, Association française de recherché sur l'histoire due cinema, Bibliotheque du film*, AFRHC, 1999, esp. plates on 190 and 302—and beyond that, evoking Duchamp's iconic *Nude Descending a Staircase*. My thanks to Richard Abel for these suggestions.

4

DREAMING IN THE ARCHIVES

The Archive is also a place of dreams.

Carolyn Steedman

At bottom, dreams are nothing other than a particular form of thinking.

Sigmund Freud

To play needs much work. But when we experience the work as play, then it is not work any more. A play is play.

Peter Brook

And here's a marvelous convenient place for our rehearsal.

Peter Quince[1]

Before the archive, before the photograph, Alan Howard's voice constitutes a "sound memory" that led me there. When I hear his voice (on tape, in another role), all of Peter Brook's *Dream* returns. I think of it still as his voice bouncing off those brilliant white walls, writing Shakespeare on them. And even without actually hearing his voice, simply conjuring it up in imagination dreams the *Dream* into being.

Two images from among those taken by Laurence Burns, whose photographs constitute an archival treasury of rehearsal—a re-dreaming of *Dream*'s beginning. The first shows Brook in a hierarchical pose at the center of what Burns calls his "holy" empty space[2]—empty, that is, except for players lying on cushions, left and right, in two curved lines that mirror one another—his hands measure its extent.

"We must," Brook writes, "prove that there will be no trickery, nothing hidden. We must open our empty hands and show that really there is nothing up our sleeves. We're holding up a white screen, and the imagination of the audience can paint on that screen what it wants."[3] Writes Marcel Jousse, "The more austere and rigid the stage, the more freedom there will be for the imagination to play. On a

FIGURE 4.1 Peter Brook presides over the *Dream* cast from the center of his "empty" space. Photograph © Laurence Burns.

bare stage, the actor is obliged to create everything, to draw everything from his own being."[4] Here, actors are the audience, place-holders for a future theatre audience and, even later, for readers—all brought together in prescient presence under the aegis of Brook-as-Prospero, playing the conjuror.[5]

FIGURE 4.2 Close-up of Oberon and Titania's hands (Alan Howard and Gemma Jones) exchanging crystal ball. Photograph © Laurence Burns.

The second image—two hands exchanging a crystal ball—exemplifies the idea of the theatrical acid test: when the play is over, what remains? "When emotion and argument are harnessed to a wish from the audience to see more clearly into itself—then something in the mind burns. The event scorches onto the memory an outline, a taste, a trace, a smell—a picture."[6] Alan Howard evokes that picture:

> The image [that] describes the complexity of the play is that it resembles a crystal ball. The center or nucleus is hollow, and all the lines contained in a sphere—diagonal, lateral, vertical, all straight, even though they're contained in or on a curved surface—go toward the center and would join up with other lines—but you can only join them in the *empty* space in the middle [my emphasis].[7]

These images complement each other in several ways: both are clearly posed and carefully composed, lending them an aura of artificiality; both encompass or frame empty space. Brook's central position and extended hands gesture towards his title, evoking a sense of suspense, as though inviting readers to imagine the performance that might take place there. The process entails comprehending that the "space, the architecture, is a kind of writing. [The] figures [are] frozen, locked into a single moment where they become a kind of scenery."[8] No trickery? The entire shot is itself a trick, one gauged to evoke belief in and desire for theatre—if only for "The most lamentable comedy, and most cruel death of Pyramus and Thisbe,"[9] the performance that pulses at *Dream*'s heart. And the image of the crystal

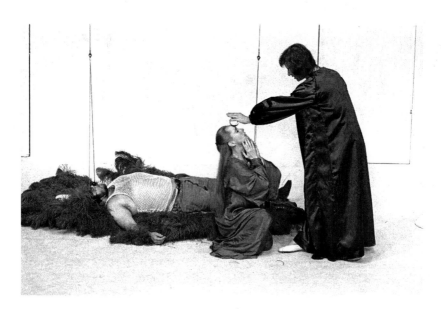

FIGURE 4.3 Crafting photograph of crystal ball. Oberon (Alan Howard) and Titania (Gemma Jones). Photograph © Laurence Burns.

ball—isolated, suspended in (empty) space, floating free—resonates with the idea of how certain moments drive to the heart of feeling, expressing something deeply mysterious.[10] The photo itself—Puck upside-down within the crystal—is a Lacanian conjuring trick. Usually, one would expect to see the photographer reflected here, but the shot also invites seeing Puck as a conjurer and marks Burns not just as complicit but as interchangeable with him, his surrogate or double. This second image appears even more extravagantly constructed when juxtaposed to a full-stage image of Oberon waking Titania—not incidentally, a shot taken from an angle that reverses the players' right- and left-stage positions.[11]

Burns describes crafting this photograph:

> On the Paris stage I got Alan/Oberon and Gemma/Titania to clasp hands slowly over the Perspex ball with me very close (I liked the "lens" effect of the Perspex ball); in one series of shots I got Puck (now played by Robert Lloyd), in his yellow balloon costume, to stand upstage and tried both Alan and Gemma holding the ball together and individually. I thought it a valid shot, though it wasn't used as a production shot as I'd forced it.

As though mimicking the posed shot of Brook opening his hands, Burns corrals and commandeers empty space. Such stills, then, are less samples than quotations, fragments that scorn logical time.[12] Given the rigorous engineering of these shots—revealing while concealing artifice—each still does and does not match either rehearsal or performance but nonetheless reads as a moment cut out of a larger time flow, a phenomenon simultaneously slipping away from posed presence and opening towards process, imagination and remembering.[13]

The story I am telling relies on and emphasizes bodies, draws upon fleshly memories. Historically dense, this collection of materials informing practice invites deciphering performance traces, signals their renewal as dreamwork—that is, it forges connections in an indefinite network.[14] A "happy disorder," writes Benjamin, who grounds his methodology on literary montage: "I needn't say anything. Merely show."[15] Photographs, however, do not describe in the same way as writing nor do they share the same temporality as text. It often requires annotations to give images a voice.[16] Those photographs generated pre-performance refer to what has not happened, are utopian, pro-active; those occurring after performance are no less utopian in their need to control and construct an authorized history. Think, for instance, of "scene of crime" graphics in murder mysteries, which enable readers to re-experience the spatiality of the past event.[17] By and large, however, these photographs are sketches, seemingly naive first beginners, remains of rehearsal's initial "try-outs," a cluster of narratives gathered from accounts by performers, onstage and offstage witnesses and spectators alike. In the case of *Dream*, offstage spectators and critics almost unanimously agree that the white squash court set offers "a giant sounding board for Shakespeare's multi-leveled language" that forces spectators to "listen to the text with a fresh ear" and that, despite the originality of the concept and individual performances, "the only thing that can be real for us is the language."[18]

Burns' photographs, however, move in another direction: faster than lightning flashes, they chronicle the developing collaboration between director, actors and photographer, figuring voice as image, as visual presence. They suggest that the visual design of the production, the choreography of actors' bodies—solo, in groups, and in relation to props, are equally significant, especially in the rehearsal process. For there is, after all, more than one Bottom in this text in terms of moves and cues—that is, Burns resembles Bottom, playing all the parts, including that of Quince, the carpenter-play-wright, as well as ventriloquizing Brook, who's doing some carpentering himself, turning rehearsal into work-play and play-work.[19]

Just looking

With Brook's permission, Burns began photographing early rehearsals, intending simply to record them. Given his previous experience with documenting theatre work, especially for the English Shakespeare Company's *Wars of the Roses*,[20] not only did he key into Brook's particular way of working but he also intuited that *this* rehearsal process was different and important precisely because of that difference.[21] The earliest rehearsals took place in the tin-roofed "TheatreGoRound" (TGR) shack that would later become the RSC's "black-box" space, The Other Place, then used primarily for props and costumes storage, but home, in 1970, for four weeks of improvisations; in the fifth week, the company moved to the Conference Hall—a different space that brought a new physicality and further emotional depths to rehearsals.[22] Burns continued taking black-and-white photographs throughout Stratford rehearsals, at the Aldwych transfer and in Paris. He describes the ambience surrounding the 1970 and 1972 rehearsals in the heat and ease of summer: The first took place:

> beside willow-tree fronds stroking the Warwickshire-scented Avon across the lane from the TheatreGoRound space (TGR); the second in the cooler, marble-like walls of *Le Mobilier national*, where lunchtime took [the company] out to the humid air of Paris, the garden strollable with only mothers and toddlers on the gravel-ash paths and dusty grass.

Insofar as the idea of "room-for-play"[23] grounds *Dream*, looking at an assemblage of photographs offers some sense of the range of Burns' work. Some images are deliberately posed, deeply fashioned; others appear to be half-posed—that is, especially when rehearsal reaches an instance of stability that permits him to do so, Burns places himself in a position to shoot. Other shots appear to have been taken on the fly, as in the images of actors playing with children—who seem unaware of the camera. In the latter two instances, Burns is analogous to a documentary filmmaker (such as Al Maysles) who lives with his subjects for a while so they comfortably accept his presence: he was, after all, Deputy Stage Manager on book for *Dream* as well as Assistant Stage Manager, responsible for running the show. Given those roles, which entailed rehearsing and re-rehearsing, he knew exactly where to position himself to get the best angle.[24] Stories upon stories; double riffing with remains.

Alan Howard's sense of the crystal ball, with its hollow nucleus, in which all lines contained within a sphere meet at the center, joining up with other lines—which can only happen in the empty space in the middle—sets the stage for the idea of the photograph as painting. Overall, Burns' work undertakes a balancing act, a fashioned collaboration with Brook and the players in terms of camera angle as well as the positions of actors in space. Speaking of his practice, Burns considers himself a musician and views the actor as a conductor who shows him the "picture moment," coaxes the image into visibility.[25] A photographer with a strong sense of visual composition, he produces unusually lucid images of rehearsal, whether capturing an instant cut out from ongoing process (at least provoking that idea) or deliberately choosing to position himself above the action, shooting down, generating abstract patterns. Put in Rob King's elegant phrase—"the abstract artistry of physical form"—to which I would add "of movement."[26]

Warming-up

Stick exercises prefaced each day of rehearsal. In the first shot, the actors are in a close circular huddle, their bamboo canes aimed at the central empty space—Brook's Gymnasium?[27] Players include Stanton, Brook's daughter Irina and Gillian Eaton. Barbara Penney sits at top right, a promptscript on her knee. In the second

FIGURE 4.4 Warm-up stick exercises, closed form. Rehearsal. Photograph © Laurence Burns.

FIGURE 4.5 Warm-up stick exercises, open form. Rehearsal. Photograph © Laurence Burns.

image, actors' bodies are spread-eagled, one leg raised to match extended arms that hold canes horizontally, as balancing rods. Positioning himself in London's Floral Street rehearsal room, its canvas floor covering taut fixed, Burns speaks of the "cloth-hung peaceful space, exploded in an instant by the work taking place": he recalls sharply catching his breath at the beauty and development of the exercises.[28] To take these photographs, Burns shinnied up a convenient leaning ladder and pointed the camera down at his subjects: the angle suggests that even though the shots seem to have been caught on the fly, they adhere to his familiar triangulated compositional design. In Simon Brook's film, *The Tightrope*, a drummer and a pianist playing the opening chords of Mozart's *The Magic Flute* lead the performers through the exercises: lessons in alertness, in links been the pure imagination and the body itself, they invite players not just to listen to the silences but also to ascertain how silence leads to the next sound, distinguishing every tempo along the way, in order to see what Brook calls "the real possible-impossible at the same time."[29] The journey these exercises undertake is "about" time and timings between each moment of time. In the first image, it is as though the players have risen up from the opening photo, filling the center with a compositional harmony that resonates with the image of the crystal ball. In the second image, the players, freed from the circle, create a different compositional harmony achieved through scattering them equidistant from one another across the floor: shot from above (as in a Busby Berkeley film), they fall into that "abstract artistry of physical form."

Helena, her bamboo cane raised in mid-gesture, shooing Hermia toward the upstage doors, observed by John Kane (smiling) and Alan Howard (adjusting his

FIGURE 4.6 Helena (Frances de la Tour) chasing Hermia (Mary Rutherford). Rehearsal. Photograph © Laurence Burns.

glasses), seated against the upstage wall. One of the few shots of women in action as well as one of the few times when stick exercises seem to have migrated from the Exercise photos, as though escaping one room for another, one world for another.

Burns' 1970 promptscript generates an all-encompassing sense of the entire space, onstage as well as offstage. The AVs (for Audio Visuals, surrogates for Fairies or

FIGURE 4.7 Titania (Gemma Jones) on feather couch; AVs (fairies) on trapezes frame her in a posed shot. Photograph © Laurence Burns.

Spirits)[30] are a means to focus particular moments. They make bird noises (or bird roars); when sounds or props are necessary, they are supplied, seemingly by magic— as when a musician holds out an alarm clock with a bell on top to awaken the lovers or when the AVs cry out to mark each eye-drop as Oberon sets a spell on Titania or throw down trousers and cap to Bottom as he surfaces from his spell-laden sleep.

An elegantly crafted shot—an instance of pure theatre. An almost over-posed shot of Titania on feather bed, wire coils with their wands frame her; four AVs aloft on trapezes, two doors open to backstage. Burns' painterly compositional eye matches Brook's minimalist painterly space, exhibits extraordinary balance through Burns' equally characteristic triangular arrangement, marked out here "by the numbers"—(1) Titania on feather couch; (2) open doors onto backstage; (3) AVs on trapezes aloft. That sense of balance is also present in the horizontal halves of the image—dark above, showing off the AVs' light costumes; light below, so that the doors opening to darkness and Titania's figure stand out.

What's fascinating here entails how the shot is structured, controlled. Brook presides over two players, extending a hand, aimed directly at both photographer and viewer, as though inviting them to conspire with him. Howard kneels at left stage; he seems contemplative, as does the standing actor (male or female?), who holds a script: their gazes appear frozen, directed neither at Brook nor at each other.

FIGURE 4.8   Peter Brook directing Alan Howard (at left frame) and androgynous player (right frame). Rehearsal image as painting. Photograph © Laurence Burns.

In a low-res version, the shot's backdrop resembles a Rothko painting; Burns' photograph, taken from an upstage position, achieves this effect, at least in part, from posing Brook and the actors at the lip of the stage and spreading a white sheet over the first few rows of theatre seats. A high-res image turns the background into a series of flattened horizontals, showing how that effect was achieved. Overall, the composition seems posed as in a museum, effectively "quickening" the shot, inviting viewers to look twice. The sense of emptiness behind the figures exerts control over them, turning them into beings rhythmically moving in space, much like notes on a musical clef. This photograph neatly documents Burns' memories of Brook clarifying and simplifying rehearsal work through a hand gesture:

> like a conductor working through a quiet intense piece, pinching thumb and forefinger ahead of and above him, as though picking a cobweb from the air. His lips seem to taste sounds; he'll hear a particular sound, head slightly on one side, listening for the right note. If a rehearsal tableau or a text-specific conclusion pleases him, he might make the sound of a camera shutter (plus a chuckle) to signal Burns. Hearing Peter talk resembles a playful osmosis; you absorb it rather than listen. It's a bit like hearing a piece of music: you absorb it through osmosis; odd words pop out, helped by his mannerisms, voice level, precision, whispering-ness, hand movements, his fingers deliberating.[31]

FIGURE 4.9 Peter Brook watching triangle of lovers. Photograph © Laurence Burns.

An exercise in theatrical geometry. In a nearly over-posed shot, Brook occupies the downstage area, seated comfortably on the floor, looking upstage at the lovers, the least important figures in the composition: they are enclosed in a "web" of Burns' and/or Brook's making, reminiscent of a panel from a medieval triptych. Brook's triangular shape is "repeated" but inverted in the balanced abstraction of the background window-like shadow.

A number of things coalesce in this image. Brook (always already observing, presiding) again occupies down left foreground watching a weird chaos made up from the detritus of performances past and unfolding here in what might be titled "Dressing Up for Peter in Paris." Paper left over from a Max Waldman photo shoot hangs aloft and is strewn willy-nilly across the floor; a group of players huddle together at right stage, facing upstage, one with a guitar, their gaze directed at two players seated on an upstage table wearing paper "dunce caps"; other players at left stage wear various costumes (many left over from the *Henry IV* plays and *Henry V*); one carries a balloon (the moon?), another a (quintessentially British) umbrella.

Wedding rehearsal, with Bottom's (Waller's) try-out of cardboard roll as surrogate cock;[32] paper from Max Waldman's photo session covers the floor; John Kane, Sara Kestleman (giggling at left-stage, in wig)[33] and others, faces obscured, watching at edges; Puck slightly right of center, smiling; player sitting on skip on back wall. This image of what I'll call Bottom Erectus is a placeholder until Hugh Keays Byrne's arm takes over as a "real" cock.

FIGURE 4.10 Peter Brook watching *Dream* cast dressing-up in "dunce caps." Photograph
© Laurence Burns.

FIGURE 4.11 Try-out of cardboard roll for the "Cock shot." Bottom Erectus (David Waller); watchers include Sara Kestleman (Titania), John Kane (Puck), Alan Howard (Oberon/Theseus). Rehearsal. Photograph © Laurence Burns.

The play's the thing: working without a net

Dream encompasses the full narrative of theatre-making, from casting through rehearsal to performance: it is, amongst other things, about acting—and illusion, centered in and growing out from the play-within-the play.[34] That event brings with it a traditional playing history framing it as a foolish comic interlude staged by a group of so-called rude mechanicals who know nothing about theatre, grounded in assumptions of nineteenth-century snobbishness and filled with one-off vaudeville routines of everything that can go wrong, a compendium of coarse acting. In this *Dream*, however, any aura of actors acting badly disappeared: instead, the play-within-the-play (its "hot ice and wondrous strange snow") became the shadow, mirror and impetus for the entire staging, its driving motor—"a microcosm of the play as a whole."[35] More precisely, Bottom, the play's chief *Dream*-er, energizes the performance, stands at its center.

After seeing Chinese acrobats, who dressed identically in white trousers and shirts, performing "astonishing feats with such ease that they vanished into anonymity, leaving in their place an impression of pure speed, of pure lightness, of pure spirit," Brook imagined staging *Dream* with a group of Shakespearean actors and Chinese acrobats. Although that proved impractical, he did borrow the costuming—white (almost) trousers and shirts for the lovers and loosely flowing brightly colored shifts for Theseus/Oberon and Hippolyta/Titania.

Hamlet Left-overs

Because he was working with actors left over from Nunn's production of *Hamlet*,[36] Brook wondered if these "inherited" players could perform such acrobatic skills. The group included nine players who were performing that play while rehearsing *Dream*: Hugh Keays Byrne (Captain, Francis, Player Mute), Frances de la Tour (Player Queen), Christopher Gable (Laertes), Alan Howard (Hamlet),[37] Terrence Hardiman (Marcellus), John Kane (Guildenstern), Barry Stanton (Gravedigger), Terrence Taplin (Horatio), David Waller (Claudius). And, by an uncanny coincidence, Laurence Burns acted as Deputy Stage Manager for both Nunn's *Hamlet* and Brook's *Dream*. One particular shot—a *Hamlet–Dream* mash-up—evidences that connection. Articulated primarily by a rack of costumes crowded onto a rail, *Hamlet* is relegated to the background and overwhelmed, even dominated, by traces of *Dream*, half way between rehearsal and performance: candles on paper plates (footlights?) flank a group of courtiers (one holds script pages), who are seated on cushions set in a semi-circle beside Alan Howard. Might this be the moment when Brook outlaws suiting the word to the action and the action to the word ("Everything is permissible save that")?[38]

How does this shot read? The windows are open, the men bare-chested, suggesting a very warm day. They look like a bunch of homeless guys: more specifically, a familiar sight—"Men At Work," words that often connote minimal work (holding up a flag, directing traffic with a hand); alternatively, they might be on lunch break. Mimicking their textual behavior, the workmen rehearsed alone (in Stratford's Methodist Hall), apart from the court; when their play was chosen,

FIGURE 4.12 Mechanics rehearsing their initial entrance: Bottom (David Waller) assigning parts, Peter Brook observing from foreground. Photograph © Laurence Burns.

they were "ordered to wait outside the door, as though they were tradesmen (which they were) and spruce themselves up before entering the presence of the 'Gentry'."[39] At the edge of right frame, which threatens to bisect him, Brook watches, the occasional passer-by. However, once a reader keys the shot to the "room-for-play" of rehearsal, it reads differently, does not represent a so-called literal reality. What's going on here? As it turned out, warm weather had nothing to do with why the players were bare-chested: Brook had asked that they remove their shoes and strip to the waist; each was to enter from a different direction, fixing attention on the variety of their appearances.[40] David Waller performs Pyramus (or Thisbe or Lion), showing off. Philip Locke (Quince) stands by an overturned oil drum, the table for his casting notes; Barry Stanton and Gwynne Lewis (Lion and Thisbe) sit on a bench. The scene begins offstage, as the noise of working (hammering) mixes with the noise of voices—the promptscript even gives Snug a line: "LU-UNCH." The workmen's appearances emphasize their fixed occupation (by contrast to the courtiers and the lovers, dressed in no-costume costumes that swerve away from theatrical tradition altogether.[41]

Props

Anything available was ripe for play: bamboo canes, plates, drums and percussion, funny noses and hats; and the scaffolding version of the set with its two levels and trapezes turned the rehearsal room into an adventure playground—an arena constructed for children, which is what the players became. Before the mad improvisation that set the first half of *Dream*, the entire cast, but particularly Alan Howard and John Kane, practiced circus "plate spinning" with made-to-order Perspex wand sticks newly invented by the Prop Workshop, and ball-point pens as

FIGURE 4.13 *Dream* cast playing with children. Photograph © Laurence Burns.

the balance tip.[42] Then, according to Howard, all would go out and buy various toys, anything associated with magic "in a simple, childlike way."[43]

Actors playing with children playing with props. Philip Locke, Ben Kingsley, Gwynne Lewis and Alan Howard joining in the adventure-playground games.[44] The compelling invitation to describe, implicit in black and white photographs (which seem incomplete), arouses a child's desire to fill out the image with his own poetry. Whereas the players are completely at ease playing with children, part of their "landscape," integrated with them, Brook often stands apart, presiding rather than joining in. Performing for children enabled the players to see what "worked" and what was over the top, repetitive, unreadable. Returning to Stratford and to a larger performance space, they developed strategies that would "increase the actors' concentration and help them project across the distance"—including trapezes, stilts, costumes' dazzling white and primary colors."[45]

A signature image: Howard spinning a disc, soon to be figured as "a little western flower,/Before, milk-white, now made purple with love's wound,/And maidens call it 'love in idleness'."[46] As the only player in every staging of Dream, he would repeat this move in 536 performances over four years.

FIGURE 4.14 Alan Howard spinning disc on perspex wand. Photograph © Laurence Burns.

FIGURE 4.15 Alan Howard and John Kane swinging on trapezes. Photograph ©
Laurence Burns.

FIGURE 4.16 Traditional ass head. Royal Shakespeare Company Collection. Photograph
courtesy of David Howells.

Bottom's Dance - David Waller

Midsummer Nights Dream RSC

Sally Jacobs '70

FIGURE 4.17 Sally Jacobs, post-performance drawing of David Waller as Bottom.
Photograph courtesy of Sally Jacobs and Shakespeare Birthplace Trust.

Howard and Kane, each on a trapeze, holding a rope. Originally, there was only
one trapeze, yet as players improvised further moves, they introduced a second
trapeze and ropes, reproducing rehearsal improvisations, as though (in part) they
ran the show.

Traditional "realistic" ass's head from RSC Collection. The angle of the photo
shoves the action to right-stage; Sally Jacobs stands directly in front of the player
wearing the slightly distressed-looking head.

Sally Jacobs' post-performance drawing of Waller doing "Bottom's Dance."
She remarks:

> One day at rehearsal, I saw [Waller] with this funny little black rubber nose
> and a funny cap....We did give him some points to put on his ears—as a
> token—and with the little nose, it worked! And the fairies strapped some
> heavy wooden clogs to his feet, to make him even more clumsy and grotesque
> and to give him height.[47]

Waller adds:

> The transformation into an ass and the rest of the rehearsing Mechanicals
> into terrified fugitives is a distillation of the games we played and the fun we
> had. Obviously, you can't turn an actor into ass, so you might just as well

not pretend you can. All you're left with is the *idea* of turning into an ass, and this is what we tried to demonstrate.

Strikingly, Waller sounds a bit like Bottom.[48]

John Kane reports that whereas the actors' usual way of working was to "do something to the play," working with Peter meant avoiding intellectualizing, rationalizing habits: "He wanted the play to *do things to us*" (my emphasis). In that vein, Kane glosses a memorable rehearsal of Titania and Bottom's "wedding":

> We whipped the play along like some frantic bobbing top until it eventually exploded during the Titania–Bottom confrontation in a welter of torn newspaper, moaning cardboard phalluses and Felix Mendelssohn. We had the sense that we were in touch with elements of the play that no discussion or "production" could have revealed. We had brushed momentarily against Peter's "secret play" and for the first time knew what we were chasing. Or thought we did. At the end, when everything quieted down, we stood and looked around at the incredible chaos—the debris—we had created. We had wrecked the entire studio. It was the first glimmer we had had of how a play can drive you.[49]

FIGURE 4.18 Throwing confetti at Bottom and Titania's "wedding." Rehearsal. Photograph © Laurence Burns.

In time, boxes filled with paper plate confetti were hung backstage on rear and side rails: several players would send a few handfuls skimming and flying. Once Oberon had "spelled" Titania and she was settled on the bower, it lifted high above the stage, where it remained for a long time, her vivid green shift and the red feathers stark against the black air of infinity, while the workmen rehearsing in the wood evolved below her, including their fearful recoil from Bottom-turned-ass. Titania aloft versus a dark "infinity" generates an afterimage—strongly resonant when the gaze bounces off a starkly white, brightly lit surface.[50]

Becoming empty

As time passed, performances became more and more simple—as well as more and more *empty*. The trapezes went, so did the ropes; Puck's stilts were gone, as were the boxes, ladders, trunks and hand props from the first scene with the workmen.[51] Paring away, eliminating much that was necessary when playing to a large proscenium space—all those devices that "increased actors' concentration and helped them project across distance," had pleased audiences and become literal *props*, as in propping up meanings.[52] Performance is made from a series of fragments, rearranged in an assemblage. That gathering then:

> immediately falls to pieces as traces and fragments of a different order, ranging from documentary photographs—those that are crafted specifically to illustrate "the look of the play"—to the memories of its participants: a progression from fragments to order and back again to fragments.[53]

In the frame

The close resonates with the opening: I imagine Burns with his arms outspread behind his camera—as though copy-catting Brook in the opening image, whose arms also are outspread, encompassing—and enclosing—the empty space.

A somewhat rare instance of Burns shooting in color. This photograph takes off from a sensuous object: here, color offers a "multisensory address"—that is, several channels or modes are mobilized. An expression of the body, yet the image "no longer *illustrates* the words; it is now the words which, structurally, are parasitic on the image."[54] Whether naming this mixing of the senses kinesthesia or synesthesia, both chime with the idea of embodied perception—the appeal of players' sensuous bodies to viewers' sensuous bodies—a bodily writing that evokes "the texture and timing of bodies in motion."[55] Basically, they're all looking upstage for safety.[56] Apart from Howard/Oberon, swinging on his single rope, whole fistfuls of paper plates and celebratory streamers are slung in the air, aimed to skim and float over the forestage. Stanton's Bottom raised on Hugh Kaeys Byrne's shoulder is being presented to the wedding celebrants: as I remember, they circle upstage a bit and then exit at the up-left-stage door following Titania; a cluster of fairies bring up the rear. Titania's "Bring him silently" cues the triumphant tableau crowned by the

FIGURE 4.19 Celebrating Bottom and Titania's "wedding." Photograph © Laurence Burns.

FIGURE 4.20 Alan Howard surrounded by items needed for *Dream*'s World Tour. Photograph © Laurence Burns.

strains of Mendelssohn's Wedding March, rising up in an extraordinary, unexpected context, crashing in at full volume. That the Mendelssohn is the only music that is recorded rather than live sets it apart so that it stands out from *Dream*'s soundscape.[57] This closing image performs, more than any other, a celebratory wedding that leaps into a radical crossing of the human bodily sensorium with the new, emphasizing accelerating movement, bodily presence. Here, writ large, the shot expresses the architecture of the play impulse—the freedom of the imagination to capture and bring into view the potentialities of all being.

Epilogue

According to Burns, Howard designed this made-to-order shot, surrounding himself with a storehouse of paraphernalia (supplied by his adoring fans).[58] He seems to be figured as a late nineteenth- or early twentieth-century British boy,[59] a kind of changeling boy, ready to tour the Commonwealth, giving the sense of his dressing room as the take-off point for touring the rest of the world as a colony. Taking a cue from the children playing with props, I like to imagine all those discarded things or objects as moving from the rehearsal spaces to the backstage dressing room, where, like Bottom, they have been "translated."[60] Howard wears a pith helmet, prepared for the tropics, a necklace of cowrie-shell beads (for trading with the natives) and tinted glasses in fashionable frames; he holds (aptly) a Players' cigarette. His robe is casually open, as though he is already feeling the heat. Two Union Jacks locate the dressing room as British territory: one on a wand calls attention to the teapot; the other decorates a paper sac or box which reads "The English Gentleman's Companion to the Colonies and Upon the Grand Tour." Material props include jars of Marmite, Fortnum and Mason's Gentleman's Relish and marmalade; a bar of Wright's coal tar soap—all signs of the suitably civilized Englishman. The dressing table holds more gear: a formal white vest, a bow tie and a pair of white spats; a cartridge belt hangs from the mirror—for meeting foreign dignitaries (or foes). Two tracts are spread across the table's surface: one reads "Keep the Home Fires Burning," the other, "There'll Always Be an England"; a copy of *Punch* and an advertisement for liquors, featuring whiskey and Drambuie, among others, a book (I imagine either a bible or a copy of *Dream*: either would mark Howard's missionary status, serving the purpose of exporting English culture to the heathen) and a framed photograph of a posh gathering—a send-off party? Print reminders of home, ready to travel: can all England be contained on a dressing table? Emphatically, yes. Here, taking over Brook's role as a conjuror, Howard fills, in miniature, his own self-reflexive empty space.

Notes

1 *A Midsummer Night's Dream*, ed. Harold F. Brooks, Arden 2 edition (London: Methuen & Co Ltd, 1979), 3.1.2–3. Freud citation from *The Interpretation of Dreams*; see also "Freud and the Scene of Writing," in Jacques Derrida, *Writing and Difference*, trans. Alan Bass (Chicago, IL: University of Chicago Press, 1978 [1967], 196–231, esp. 211–215.
2 Laurence Burns email (September 18, 2014).
3 "In order to make *nothingness* around the work, the white walls were not there to state something but to *eliminate* something; on such a nothingness, something can be conjured up—and then made to disappear." Peter Brook, *The Empty Space* (New York: Atheneum, 1968), 97, 25, 32.

4 Marcel Jousse, *L'Anthropologie du geste* (Paris: Resma, 1969), 90; see also Jacques Copeau, *Registres*, vol. 1 of *Appels* (Paris: Gallimard, 1974).

5 Sally Jacobs considers the set as "a contained space [that] gave us a sense of distance, but at the same time it was very intimate." See "Designing the Dream: From Tantras to Tunics," in *Peter Brook's Production of William Shakespeare's A Midsummer Night's Dream for The Royal Shakespeare Company: Authorized Acting edition*, ed. Glenn Loney (Chicago, IL: Dramatic Publishing Company and The Royal Shakespeare Company of Stratford-upon-Avon, 1974), 46–47.

6 Brook, *Empty Space*, 123–124.

7 See Alan Howard, "On Keeping the Dream From Becoming a Nightmare," *Authorized Acting*, 39; see also Brook, *Empty Space*, 136.

8 I draw from "Looking Back: A Conversation About Presence, 2006," Nick Kaye and Tim Etchells in dialogue, *Archaeologies of Presence: Art, Performance and the Persistence of Being*, ed. Gabriella Giannachi et al. (London and New York: Routledge, 2012), 190–192. See also Gaston Bachelard's notion of scenography as "active performance" in *The Poetics of Space*, trans. Maria Jolas (New York: Orion Press, 1964), 141.

9 *Dream*. Arden 2 edition, 1.2.11–12.

10 Especially, according to Brook, at Puck's last speech: "the end of it is . . . tantalizingly close to something secret and mysterious." See David Selbourne, *The Making of A Midsummer Night's Dream: An Eye-Witness Account of Peter Brook's Production From First Rehearsal to First Night* (London: Methuen London, 1982), 15, 19.

11 The 1970 promptscript, made by Laurence Burns, glosses the shot: "At 'See as thou was't wont to see,' O strokes T's neck with wand"; at "Be as thou was't," "He's slowly touching the ball to Titania, now kneeling to him, head up, not seeing him yet; as he reaches 'force and blessed power,' he rolls the ball slowly down her forehead and at 'Now my Titania' he rolls the ball down her nose, then releases it for her cupped hands to catch."

12 See Roland Barthes, "The Third Meaning," *Image/Music/Text*, trans. Stephen Heath (New York: Hill and Wang, 1977), 67–68.

13 I draw on Carolyn Steedman, *Dust: The Archive and Cultural History* (New Brunswick, NJ: Rutgers University Press, 2002), 67.

14 This section is indebted to conversations with Richard Abel.

15 See Walter Benjamin, *The Arcades Project*, trans. Howard Eiland and Kevin McLaughlin (Cambridge, MA and London: Belknap Press of Harvard University Press, 1999), 460 [N1a, 8]; and "Unpacking My Library: A Talk About Book Collecting," in *Selected Writings* vol. 2, Part 2, 1931–1934, trans. Rodney Livingston and Others, eds. Michael W. Jennings, Howard Eiland, and Gary Smith (Cambridge, MA and London: Belknap Press of Harvard, 1999), 486–493.

16 See Mike Pearson and Michael Shanks, *Theatre/Archaeology* (London: Routledge, 2001), 43. See also Walter Benjamin, *Selected Writings*, Volume 2.2, 1927–1934. Ed. Michael W. Jennings (Cambridge, MA: Belknap Press of Harvard, 1999), 576.

17 Pearson and Shanks, *Theatre/Archaeology*, 58–59. See also Gay McAuley, *Space in Performance: Making Meaning in the Theatre* (Ann Arbor, MI: University of Michigan Press, 2000).

18 See, for instance, Jack Kroll, "Placing the Living Shakespeare Before Us," *New York Times* (February 7, 1971), D1; Clive Barnes, "Peter Brook's *A Midsummer Night's Dream*," *New York Times* (January 21, 1971); Peter Fiddick, *Midsummer Night's Dream*, *Guardian* (August 28, 1970).

19 See Pearson and Shanks, *Theatre/Archaeology*, 57–58; 1970 promptscript, 69; for the work/play move, see Brook, *Empty Space*, 141, reproduced in the Epigraph.

20 Catalogued in Chapter 2. Before working on either *Wars* or *Dream*, Burns had acted as Assistant Stage Manager with a theatre company, Century Theatre, based in Preston, that later became Theatre 69.

21 Two Stratford journalists also documented rehearsals at an open photo call. Joe Cocks shot from several rows back in the stalls, and Tom Holt, who set up a tripod at front center of the dress circle, generated a very "toppy" view of the stage floor, accentuated by its own rake, instead of opting for the drama of a straight auditorium shot. Whereas

Cocks offered black and white shots for his local shop sales, Holt always shot in color. The Shakespeare Centre Library archives both photographers' work.

22 See Selbourne, *Making*, citing Brook, 165. Selbourne wrote his book a decade after his observation.

23 I borrow from Miriam Bratu Hansen's title: "Room-for-Play: Benjamin's Gamble with Cinema," *October* 109 (Summer, 2004), 3–45.

24 Burns, Abel and myself occupy various positions along a continuum of looking. Burns and I have seen *Dream* in performance and so bring along considerable baggage to thinking—fragments that are difficult to push away. Abel comes to these images as an outsider, with the gaze of a cinema historian. The stories we tell about these photographs differ at times; at others, they dovetail rather precisely.

25 Laurence Burns email, September 15, 2014.

26 My thanks to Richard Abel for alerting me to King's work.

27 See Roland Barthes, "The Diseases of Costume," trans. Richard Howard, in *Critical Essays* (Evanston, IL: Northwestern University Press, 1977), 41–50; see also Simon Brook, dir. *Sur un fil/ The Tightrope* DVD. 2012, French and English.

28 Laurence Burns email (April 23, 2014).

29 See Brook, *Sur un Fil/ The Tightrope*.

30 On fairies and spirits, see Brook, *The Shifting Point: Theatre, Film, Opera 1946–1987* (New York: Harper and Row, 1987), esp. 96–97.

31 Laurence Burns email (May 17, 2013).

32 Brook speaks of the ass as a "'copulatory emblem,' of the Golden Ass as a 'walking cock'." See Selbourne, *Making*, quoting Brook, 5.

33 Original silver and copper wire wigs for Oberon and Titania were cut. See Michael Bogdanov, *Shakespeare: The Director's Cut: Essays on the Tragedies, Comedies and Histories* (Edinburgh: Capercaillie Books, 2013), 76.

34 On the idea of play as a free activity—and source of freedom, in as much as it is set apart from ordinary or everyday life—see Johan Huizinga, *Homo Ludens: A Study of the Play Element in Culture* (Boston, MA: Beacon Press, 1955).

35 Selbourne, *Making*, citing Brook, 3.

36 See Brook, *Threads of Time: A Memoir* (New York and London: Methuen Drama, 1998), 149.

37 Howard was the only player who was in the first and every subsequent production. One hundred and twelve performances took place in six cities throughout the United States and Canada; the 1971 Aldwych transfer saw ninety stagings, including those in Europe, ending in March 1972; forty-seven performances took place in Los Angeles and twenty-three in San Francisco before *Dream* traveled to Japan and Australia. See Selbourne, *Making*, xxviii.

38 See John Kane, "Plotting," *Authorized Acting*, 59. See also Barthes, "The Third Meaning: Research Notes on Some Eisenstein Stills," in *Image/Music/Text*, trans. Stephen Heath (New York: Hill and Wang, 1978), esp. 67.

39 Kane, "Plotting," *Authorized Acting*, 59, 61.

40 See Selbourne, *Making*, citing Brook, 49.

41 *Dream* straddles staging a moment in cultural history that coincides with "hippie" culture. Roger Howells (interview, Summer 2013) lists some borrowings: The Beatles and their meeting with the Maharishi, the use of a sitar, "flower power," appeal to the young—especially with the tie-dyed costumes for the lovers, the informal dressing-down.

42 Combines notes from Kane, "Plotting," *Authorized Acting*, 58 with his annotations in Michael Kustow, *Peter Brook: A Biography* (New York: St. Martin's Press, 2005), 188.

43 "Alan Howard: On Keeping a Dream From Becoming a Nightmare," *Authorized Acting*, 38.

44 See Benjamin, "Old Forgotten Children's Books," in *Selected Writings*, vol. 1, 1913–1926, trans. Rodney Livingstone (Cambridge, MA: Harvard University Press, 1996), 411–412.

When children think up stories, they are like theatre producers who refuse to be bound by "sense". Give children four or five specific words and ask them to make a sentence, and the most amazing prose comes to light. At a stroke, the words throw on their costumes and in the twinkling of an eye they are caught up in a battle, love scenes, or a brawl. This is how children write their stories; it is also how they read them.

45 See Brook, *Threads of Time*, 151.
46 *Dream*, Arden 2 edition, 2.1, 166–168.
47 Jacobs, "Designing the Dream," *Authorized Acting*, 51.
48 Waller cited in Croyden interview, *Authorized Acting*, 27.
49 Combines notes from *Authorized Acting*, 26, 58 with John Kane's annotations from Kustow, *Peter Brook*, 188.
50 On afterimages, see Joshua Yumibe, *Moving Color: Early Film, Mass Culture and Modernism* (New Brunswick, NJ and London: Rutgers University Press, 2012), 17, 21–22.
51 Many cuts occurred during the second stage of rehearsals for the world tour. See Barbara Penney, "Staging the Dream," *Authorized Acting*, 95.
52 See Penney, "Staging," 151.
53 See Pearson and Shanks, *Theatre/Archaeology*, 55.
54 See Barthes, "The Photographic Message," in *Image/Music/Text*, trans. Stephen Heath (New York: Hill and Wang, 1978), 25–26.
55 See Susan Leigh Foster, *Choreographing History* (Bloomington, IN: Indiana University Press, 1995), 9, 13, 15. Configuring connections among networks marks associations between physical experience and conceptual thought. See George Lakoff and Mark Johnson, *Philosophy in the Flesh: The Embodied Mind and Its Challenge to Western Thought* (New York: Basic Books, 1999), 95–97, 102–104; on color, 105–106. Burns much prefers shooting in black and white; color, he claims, leaches out drama.
56 Burns took this photograph at the Aldwych specifically for a *Theatre de ville* photo call (email, September 26, 2012).
57 See Penney, "Staging," 151.
58 Howard asked Burns to make copies of this photograph for his fans, some of whom had amassed the paraphernalia in the shot.
59 See, for instance, *The Union Jack*, a halfpenny magazine released in the last decade of the nineteenth century: *Pluck* published tales of daring deeds in Afghanistan, India and Egypt. See *Penny Dreadfuls and Comics*, catalogue of an exhibition from the Library of Oldenburg University, West Germany at the Bethnal Green Museum of Childhood, June–October 1983, 52–53.
60 *Dream*, Arden 2 edition, 3.1.114.

LOOKING FORWARD

An epilogue

Looking forward entails looking back, gathering dissimilar items of material "stuff" from the RSC Collection as a model for doing archival work. What form might it take? I have in mind something like an installation, in the sense that Peter Greenaway's *Prospero's Books* brings together images from his film of Shakespeare's *Tempest* with marginalia, commentary and drawings, held in tension though not necessarily brought into synthesis.[1] How, I want to ask, do these selected remains— properties, set models, costumes—take on meanings? What stories does each tell?

Standing out from among an armory of Henry Irving's weapons—his name and role etched on each blade—are Richard Burton's sword from his 1951 Henry V and the boar sword which Christopher Ravenscroft's Richmond used to kill Antony Sher's Richard III. These carry an enclosed resonance, turning back on themselves—that is, each gains meaning in relation to the actor's name and role. The same might be said of a curiously wrought lantern, for its meaning has to do with the myths that have enhanced its aura over time. Supposedly used by a murderer, Irving carried it onstage when he played Hamlet. Did he pick it up or was he given it by an admirer? Did he, like Gielgud, who gave his gift of Edmund Kean's sword to Olivier, pass the lantern to another, giving it a social dynamism as it moved across time and space from one actor to another? In a slightly different category, a set model for a 1978 *Coriolanus* starring Alan Howard, borne aloft, his face and parts of his costume bloodied, evokes a second-order performance, a performance-about-performance that functions not just as a mnemonic of my presence but also as a means of integrating surviving fragments—the model's miniature world, a Joseph Cornell-like box that precedes performance surprisingly become its means of survival.[2] Or consider the lion mask from Brook's 1970 *Dream*: a flea market object, something remaining from a jumble sale (Who would buy it?). Obviously and lovingly made, it's tied to performance memory: the marks of decay render its life history in material terms, giving it an extraordinary "thing-ness"—a child's idea of a lion. What to say of an anorak worn by David Tennant as Hamlet? A kind of ambiguous temporality marks it; as costume, it bears signs of hard use—a broken zipper, dirt and sweat on the lining and the turned-back cuffs; unlike many objects, this could come right out of the archive and be put to work in the everyday world, its poetics absorbed by narratives of actor's identity and ordinary fact.

My primary example, a pair of shoes, has perhaps the richest contextual histories of all, beginning with their connection to Antony Sher, who wore them as Lear's Fool, taking them as matter-of-fact. Tough shoes: photographed pointing right stage, the right shoe slightly ahead of the left, as though the feet they enclosed were walking forward. They bear heavy caps: not for tap or soft-shoe dancing, these shoes mean business. Their theatrical narrative leads from Fool to Charlie Chaplin and to the fictional and real tramps who are his ancestors, played out and come to rest on a real-life (paper) stage in Walker Evans' 1936 photograph of "Floyd Burroughs' Work Shoes, Hale County, Alabama," reproduced in *Let Us Now Praise Famous Men*. Although theatrical narratives may serve as provocative counterpoints to real-life ordinary facts, in the archive, fiction and truth mingle, as though taking pleasure in the stories they reveal.

Only one potential model for archive work, my installation offers an incentive to sketch out further studies. What other forms might continue the project of writing a materialist historiography which sutures past to present? Writing a genealogy of one particular performance, tracing how conjunctions between archived object and performance work might be read through one or several

FIGURE 5.1 Clown Shoes, worn by Antony Sher as Fool in *King Lear*, Royal Shakespeare Company, 1982, dir. Adrian Noble. Royal Shakespeare Company Collection. Photograph © Richard Abel.

categories of remains. Or writing across the repertoire of performances that make up a season for a particular company or a particular theatre. Or writing about only one category of remains: here, costumes perhaps provide the broadest spectrum. In the archive, where a costume hangs, naked, on a padded hanger—a trace torn away from performance, no longer quite life yet not death, registering simultaneously the decay of performance and its evocative afterlife—what reading perspective does it promote? What is the ontological status of a frame without a body that still evokes the performer-in-role who once occupied it? Whether in the theatre or the archive, costume insists on the body and its desires. Costume *is* subject, a material mode of performance praxis that defines and annotates role. Two costumes from different eras—Vivien Leigh's robes for her post-war 1955 Lady Macbeth, designed by Roger Furse; Judi Dench's costume, pulled from stock, for her 1977 Lady—offer a case in point. Leigh wore an emerald green underdress, overlaid with an encasing cloak, laced by golden strappings encircling her shoulders and outlining the coat's flared folds, a dress that evokes a long tradition of fabulous costumes as a re-enactment of Empire. Some twenty years later, Dench's Lady wears not a costume but clothes—an ascetic garment that covers her body, de-emphasizing her sexuality; a simple scarf wraps her head, turning her into a peasant: Lady M as Mother Courage. Material and weight imprint themselves on performance possibility: whereas Leigh's elaborated elegance evinces statuesque, static performance style, Dench's minimalist attire, weighing just under two pounds in contrast to Leigh's twelve, enables her to assert a remarkable physical performance.[3]

Placed at the end of this display of material artifacts, I imagine a mirror, see myself reflected there or perhaps having passed through, leading others to play in many more archives of theatrical remains—carrying away a prop, wearing a costume, animating a photograph, adding annotations to a rehearsal script. Luring leftovers to come alive.

Notes

1 Michael Pearson and Michael Shanks, *Theatre/Archaeology* (London and New York: Routledge, 2001), 58–59; 63–65.
2 See Peter Greenaway's curatorial practices and gallery installations, which draw dissimilar objects and live performers-as-exhibits into juxtaposition, thus challenging conventional museum codes of classification and display—see *The Tempest* and *Flying Out of This World* (Chicago, IL: Chicago University Press, 1994). See also John Onians, ed. *Sight and Insight: Essays on Art and Culture in Honor of E.H. Gombrich at 85* (London: Phaidon Press, 1993).
3 See my "Shopping in the Archives: Material Memories," 151–152.

BIBLIOGRAPHY

Adams, John, *The Impossible Itself*. Documentary film of San Quentin performances of *Godot*. 2010.

Auerbach, Nina, *Ellen Terry, Player in Her Time* (New York: W.W. Norton, 1987).

——, "Introduction: Ellen Terry's Lost Lives," in *Ellen Terry: Spheres of Influence*, ed. Katherine Cockin (London: Pickering and Chatto, 2011).

Auslander, Phillip, "Boal, Blau, Brecht: The Body," in Auslander, *From Acting to Performance: Essays in Modernism and Postmodernism* (London and New York: Routledge, 1997).

——, "The Performativity of Performance Documentation," *Performing Arts Journal (PAJ)* 84.3 (2006), 1–10.

Bachelard, Gaston, *The Poetics of Space*, trans. Maria Jolas (Boston, MA: Beacon Press, 1994).

Baldwin, Fanny, "E.W. Godwin and Design for the Theater," in *E.W. Godwin: Aesthetic Movement Architect and Designer*, ed. Susan Weber Soros (New Haven, CT: Yale University Press, 1999).

Bancroft, Squire, *Mr. & Mrs. Bancroft On and Off the Stage, Written by Themselves* (London: R. Bentley and Son, 1888).

Bancroft, Squire and Marie Bancroft, "Four Failures," in *The Bancrofts: Recollections of Sixty Years . . . with Portraits and Illustrations* (New York: E.P. Dutton and Co., 1909).

Barba, Eugenio, "Four Spectators," *The Drama Review (TDR)* 34.1 (1990), 96–101.

Barnes, Clive, "Peter Brook's *A Midsummer Night's Dream*" *New York Times* (January 21, 1971).

Barthes, Roland, "The Diseases of Costume," trans. Richard Howard, in *Critical Essays* (Evanston, IL: Northwestern University Press, 1977).

——, *Image/Music/Text*, trans. Stephen Heath (New York: Hill and Wang, 1977).

——, "The Grain of the Voice," in *Image/Music/Text*, trans. Stephen Heath (New York: Hill and Wang, 1977), 179–189.

——, "The Photographic Message," in *Image/Music/Text*, trans. Stephen Heath (New York: Hill and Wang, 1978), 15–31.

——, "The Third Meaning: Research Notes on Some Eisenstein Stills," in *Image/Music/Text*, trans. Stephen Heath (New York: Hill and Wang, 1977), 52–68.

——, *Camera Lucida: Reflections on Photography*, trans. Richard Howard (New York: Hill and Wang, 1981).

Baudrillard, Jean, *Seduction*, trans. Brian Singer (New York: St. Martin's Press, 1996).

Beckett, Samuel, *Waiting for Godot* (New York: Grove Press, 1954).

——, *Endgame* (New York: Grove Press, 1968).

Benedetti, Jean, *Stanislavski: An Introduction* (London and New York: Routledge, 2004).

Benjamin, Walter, "Theses on the Philosophy of History, VI," in *Illuminations*, trans. Harry Zohn, 1955 rpt. (New York: Schocken Books, 1969).

——, *Selected Writings*, vol. 1, 1913–1926, trans. Rodney Livingstone (Cambridge, MA: Harvard University Press, 1996).

——, "Old Forgotten Children's Books," in *Selected Writings*, vol. 1, 1913–1926, trans. Rodney Livingstone (Cambridge, MA: Harvard University Press, 1996), 411–412.

——, *The Arcades Project*, trans. Howard Eiland and Kevin McLaughlin (Cambridge, MA: Harvard University Press, 1999).

——, *Selected Writings*, vol. 2, part 2, 1931–1934, ed. Michael W. Jennings et al. (Cambridge, MA: Belknap Press of Harvard, 1999).

——, "Unpacking My Library: A Talk About Book Collecting," in *Selected Writings* vol. 2, Part 2, 1931–1934, trans. Rodney Livingston and Others, eds. Michael W. Jennings, Howard Eiland, and Gary Smith (Cambridge, MA and London: Belknap Press of Harvard, 1999), 486–493.

——, "Little History of Photography," in *Selected Writings* vol. 2, Part 2, 1931–1934, trans. Rodney Livingston and Others, eds. Michael W. Jennings, Howard Eiland, and Gary Smith (Cambridge, MA and London: Belknap Press of Harvard, 1999), 507–530.

——, "Excavation and Memory," in *Selected Writings* vol. 2, Part 2, 1931–1934, trans. Rodney Livingston and Others, eds. Michael W. Jennings, Howard Eiland, and Gary Smith (Cambridge, MA and London: Belknap Press of Harvard, 1999), 576.

——, "Hashish in Marseille," in *Selected Writings* vol. 2, Part 2, 1931–1934, trans. Rodney Livingston and Others, eds. Michael W. Jennings, Howard Eiland, and Gary Smith (Cambridge, MA and London: Belknap Press of Harvard, 1999), 673–679.

——, "The Author as Producer," in *Selected Writings* vol. 2, Part 2, 1931–1934, trans. Rodney Livingston and Others, eds. Michael W. Jennings, Howard Eiland, and Gary Smith (Cambridge, MA and London: Belknap Press of Harvard, 1999), 768–782.

Berger, John, *Another Way of Telling* (New York: Vintage International, 1995).

——, *Bento's Sketchbook* (New York: Pantheon Books, 2011).

Bernhardt, Sarah, "Men's Roles as Played by Women," *Harper's Bazaar* 33.50 (December 15, 1900), 2113–2115.

Bernstein, Robin, "Dances with Things: Material Culture and the Performance of Race," *Social Text* 27.4 (2009), 67–94.

Bingham, Madeleine, *"The Great Lover": The Life and Art of Herbert Beerbohm Tree* (London: Hamish Hamilton, 1978).

Boaden, James, *Memoirs of the Life of John Philip Kemble, esq., including a History of the Stage from the Time of Garrick to the Present Period*, vol. 1 (London: Longman, Hurst, Rees, Orme, Brown and Green, 1825).

Boal, Augusto, *Theatre of the Oppressed*, trans. Charles A. and Maria-Odilia Leal McBridge (New York: Theatre Communications Group, 1978 [1973 in Spanish]).

Bogdanov, Michael, *Shakespeare: The Director's Cut: Essays on the Tragedies, Comedies and Histories* (Edinburgh: Capercaillie Books, 2013).

Bogdanov, Michael, and Michael Pennington, *The English Shakespeare Company: The Story of "the Wars of the Roses," 1986–1989* (London: Nick Hern Books, 1990).

Bolton, Terry and Deborah Bolton, *Before the Movies* (New Barnet, UK: John Libby Publishing, 2014; Bloomington, IN: Indiana University Press, 2014).

Bond, Edward, *Bingo* (New York: Hill and Wang, 1975).

Booth, Michael R, *Victorian Spectacular Theatre 1850–1910* (London: Routledge & Kegan Paul, 1981).

——, "Pictorial Acting and Ellen Terry," in *Shakespeare and the Victorian Stage*, ed. Richard Foulkes (Cambridge: Cambridge University Press, 1986), 78–86.

Bradley, David, *From Text to Performance in the Elizabethan Theatre: Preparing the Play for the Stage* (Cambridge: Cambridge University Press, 1992).

Bradley, Harriet, "The Seductions of the Archive," *History of the Human Sciences* 12.2 (1999), 107–122.

Brook, Peter, *The Empty Space* (New York: Atheneum, 1968).

——, *Les Voies de la Creation Theatrale* XIII, ed. G. Banu (Paris: Editions du Centre National de la Recherche Scientifique, 1985).

——, *The Shifting Point: Theatre, Film, Opera 1946–1987* (New York: Harper and Row, 1987).

——, *Threads of Time: A Memoir* (New York and London: Methuen Drama, 1998).

Brook, Simon, Dir. *Sur un fil / The Tightrope* DVD. 2012, French and English.

Brooks, Harold F., ed. *A Midsummer Night's Dream*, Arden 2 edition (London: Methuen, 1979).

Brown, John Russell, ed. *The Merchant of Venice*, Arden 2 edition (London: Methuen, 1955; rpt. 1969).

Bufalini, Leonardo, *Roma al tempo di Giulio III; la pianta di Roma di Leonardo Bufalini del 1551.* Franz Ehrle, Biblioteca apostolica vaticana (Rome: Danese, 1911).

Burns, Laurence, Promptscript, *A Midsummer Night's Dream* (1970).

——, Private communications, 2005–2015.

Calbi, Maurizio, "'In States Unborn and Accents Yet Unknown': Spectral Shakespeare in Paolo and Vittorio Taviani's *Cesare deve morire* (*Caesar Must Die*)," *Shakespeare Bulletin* 32.2 (2014), 235–253.

Calhoun, Joshua, "The Word Made Flax: Cheap Bibles, Textual Corruption, and the Poetics of Paper," *PMLA* 126.2 (2011), 327–344.

Camille, Michael and Adrian Rifkin, eds. *Other Objects of Desire: Collectors and Collecting Queerly* (Oxford: Blackwell, 2001).

Carlson, Marvin, *The Haunted Stage: The Theatre as Memory Machine* (Ann Arbor, MI: University of Michigan Press, 2003).

de Certeau, Michel, "Reading as Poaching," *The Practice of Everyday Life*, trans. Steven Rendell [1984] (Berkeley, CA: University of California Press, 1988).

Chekhov, Michael, *On Theatre and the Art of Acting*, Working Arts Library. Orig. *On the Technique of Acting*, ed. Mel Gordon (New York: Harper Perennial, 1991).

Coates, Paul, ed. *Lucid Dreams: The Films of Krzysztof Kieslowski* (Wiltshire, UK: Flicks Books, 1999).

Cockin, Katherine, "Introduction: Ellen Terry's Lost Lives," in *Ellen Terry: Spheres of Influence*, ed. Katherine Cockin (London: Pickering and Chatto, 2011).

Cohen, Jonathan D. and Jonathan W. Schooler, eds. *Scientific Approaches to Consciousness.* Carnegie Mellon Symposia on Cognition (Mahwah, NJ: L. Erlbaum Associates, 1997).

Comyns-Carr, Alice, *J. Comyns Carr; Stray Memories, by His Wife* (London: Macmillan and Co., 1920).

Copeau, Jacques, *Registres*, vol. 1 of *Appels* (Paris: Gallimard, 1974).

Croyden, Margaret, "Interview," in *Peter Brook's Production of William Shakespeare's A Midsummer Night's Dream for The Royal Shakespeare Company: Authorized Acting Edition*, ed. Glenn Loney (Chicago, IL: Dramatic Publishing Company and The Royal Shakespeare Company of Stratford-upon-Avon, 1974), 25–34 *passim*.

Damasio, Antonio R, *The Feeling of What Happens: Body and Emotion in the Making of Consciousness* (New York and London: Harcourt Brace & Company, 1999).

Daniell, David, ed. *Julius Caesar*, Arden 3 edition (London: Thomas Nelson and Sons, 1998).

Dargis, Manohla, "Friends, Romans, Countrymen, All Brought to Life by Inmates," *New York Times* (February 5, 2013). http://www.nytimes.com/2013/02/06/movies/caesar-must-die-by-paolo-and-vittorio-taviani.html, accessed August 6, 2015.

deCordova, Richard, *Picture Personalities: The Emergence of the Star System in America* (Champaign, IL: University of Illinois Press, 1990).

Derrida, Jacques, "Freud and the Scene of Writing," in *Writing and Difference*, trans. Alan Bass (Chicago, IL: University of Chicago Press, 1978), 196–231.

——, *Margins of Philosophy*, trans. Alan Bass (Brighton: Harvester Press, 1982).

——, *The Postcard: From Socrates to Freud and Beyond*, trans. Alan Bass (Chicago, IL: University of Chicago Press, 1987).

——, *Archive Fever: A Freudian Impression*, trans. Eric Presnowitz (Chicago, IL: University of Chicago Press, 1998).

Dorney, Kate, "Archives," *Contemporary Theatre Review* 23.1 (2013), 8–10.

Enterline, Lynne, *Shakespeare's Schoolroom: Rhetoric, Discipline, Emotion* (Philadelphia, PA: University of Pennsylvania Press, 2012).

Etchells, Tim, Gabriella Giannachi and Nick Kaye, "Looking Back: a Conversation about Presence, 2006," in *Archaeologies of Presence: Art, Performance and the Persistence of Being*, ed. Gabriella Giannachi, with Nick Kaye and Michael Shanks (London and New York: Routledge, 2012), 183–194.

Farge, Arlette. *The Allure of the Archives*, trans. Thomas Scott-Railton (New Haven, CT: Yale University Press, 2013).

Fiddick, Peter, *Midsummer Night's Dream, Guardian* (August 28, 1970).

Fischer-Lichte, Erika, "Appearing as Embodied Mind: Defining a Weak, a Strong and a Radical Concept of Presence," in *Archaeologies of Presence: Art, Performance and the Persistence of Being*, ed. Gabriella Giannachi, with Nick Kaye and Michael Shanks (London and New York: Routledge, 2012), 103–118.

Foakes, R.A, ed. *King Lear*, Arden 2 edition (Walton-on-Thames: Thomas Nelson and Sons, 1997).

Foster, Susan Leigh, ed. "An Introduction to Moving Bodies," in Foster, *Choreographing History* (Bloomington, IN: Indiana University Press, 1995), 3–24.

——, "Choreographies of Gender," *Signs: Journal of Women in Culture and Society* 24.1 (1998), 1–33.

——, *Choreographing Empathy: Kinesthesia in Performance* (London and New York: Routledge, 2011).

Foucault, Michel, *The Order of Things: An Archaeology of the Human Sciences* [1966] (Paris: Gallimard, 1996).

Freud, Sigmund, *The Interpretation of Dreams*, trans. and ed. James Strachey (New York: Basic Books, 1955).

——, "Notes on the Mystic Writing Pad," trans. James Strachey et al., in *The Standard Edition of the Complete Psychological Works of Sigmund Freud*, vol. 19, ed. James Strachey (London: Hogarth Press and Institute of Psycho-Analysis, 1961), 225–232.

Giannachi, Gabriella, Nick Kaye and Michael Shanks (eds.), *Archaeologies of Presence: Art, Performance and the Persistence of Being* (London and New York: Routledge, 2012).

Gil Harris, Jonathan, *Untimely Matter in the Time of Shakespeare* (Philadelphia, PA: University of Pennsylvania Press, 2009).

Godwin, Edward W., F.S.A., "The Architecture and Costume of *The Merchant of Venice*," *The Mask*, ed. Edward Gordon Craig, 1–3 (1908–1911), 75–82.

——, "A Lecture on Dress," *The Mask* 6.4 (1914), 335–352.

Greenaway, Peter, *Flying Out of this World* (Chicago, IL: Chicago University Press, 1994).

Greg, W.W, *Two Elizabethan Stage Abridgements: The Battle of Alcazar & Orlando Furioso: An Essay in Critical Bibliography* (Oxford: Clarendon Press, 1923).

Handke, Peter, *Offending the Audience*, in *Plays I* (London: Methuen, 1997).

Hansen, Miriam Bratu, "Room-for-Play: Benjamin's Gamble with Cinema," *October* 109 (Summer 2004), 3–45.

Herold, Niels, "Movers and Losers: Shakespeare in Charge and Shakespeare Behind Bars," in *Native Shakespeares: Indigenous Appropriations on a Global Stage*, ed. Craig Dionne and Parmita Kapadia (London: Ashgate, 2008), 153–169.

Heywood, Thomas, *Apology for Actors* (1612), rpt. (London: Shakespeare Society, 1841).

Hodgdon, Barbara, "Rehearsal Process as Critical Practice: John Barton's 1978 *Love's Labour's Lost*," *Theatre History Studies* (January 1, 1988), 29–30.

——, *The Shakespeare Trade* (Philadelphia, PA: University of Pennsylvania Press, 1998).

——, "Photography, Theater, Mnemonics; or, Thirteen Ways of Looking at a Still," in *Theorizing Practice: Redefining Theatre History*, ed. W.B. Worthen and Peter Holland (London: Palgrave Macmillan, 2003), 88–119.

——, "Shopping in the Archives: Material Memories," in *Shakespeare, Memory and Performance*, ed. Peter Holland (Cambridge: Cambridge University Press, 2006), 135–167.

——, "Material Remains at Play," *Theatre Journal* 64.3 (October 2012), 373–388.

Hogan, Patrick Colm, "Tragic Lives: On the Incompatibility of Law and Ethics," *College English* 35.3 (Summer 2008), 1–29.

Howard, Alan, "On Keeping the Dream From Becoming a Nightmare," in *Peter Brook's Production of William Shakespeare's A Midsummer Night's Dream for The Royal Shakespeare Company: Authorized Acting Edition*, ed. Glen Loney (Chicago, IL: Dramatic Publishing Company and The Royal Shakespeare Company of Stratford-upon-Avon, 1974), 35–44.

Hughes, Alan, *Henry Irving, Shakespearean* (Cambridge: Cambridge University Press, 1981).

Huizinga, Johan, *Homo Ludens: A Study of the Play Element in Culture* (Boston, MA: Beacon Press, 1955).

Humphreys, A.R., ed. *King Henry IV, Part 2* (London: Methuen and Co., 1977).

Jackson, Heather, *Marginalia: Readers Writing in Books* (New Haven, CT: Yale University Press, 2001).

Jacobs, Sally, "Designing the Dream: From Tantras to Tunics," in *Peter Brook's Production of William Shakespeare's A Midsummer Night's Dream for The Royal Shakespeare Company: Authorized Acting Edition*, ed. Glen Loney (Chicago, IL: Dramatic Publishing Company and The Royal Shakespeare Company of Stratford-upon-Avon, 1974), 45–52.

Johnson, Marilyn, *Lives in Ruins: Archaeologists and the Seductive Lure of Human Rubble* (New York: Harper, 2014).

Jousse, Marcel, *L'Anthropologie du geste* (Paris: Resma, 1969).

Kane, John, "Plotting with Peter," in *Peter Brook's Production of William Shakespeare's A Midsummer Night's Dream for The Royal Shakespeare Company: Authorized Acting Edition*, ed. Glen Loney (Chicago, IL: Dramatic Publishing Company and The Royal Shakespeare Company of Stratford-upon-Avon, 1974), 53–64.

Kastan, David, ed. *King Henry IV, Part 1*, Arden 3 edition (London: Thomson Learning, 2002).

Kean, Charles, *Shakespeare's play of The Merchant of Venice, arranged for representation at the Princess's Theatre, with historical and explanatory notes by Charles Kean, as first performed on Saturday, June 12, 1858* (London: John K. Chapman and Co., 1858).

Kemp, Rick, *Embodied Acting: What Neuroscience Tells Us About Performance* (London and New York: Routledge, 2012).

Kickasola, Joseph, "Decalogue V and A Short Film about Killing," in Kickasola, *The Films of Krzysztof Kieslowski: The Liminal Image* (New York: Continuum, 2004).

Knight, Jeffrey Todd, "Making Shakespeare's Books: Assembly and Intertextuality in the Archives," *Shakespeare Quarterly* 60.3 (2009), 304–340.

Knowles, Ric, *Reading the Material Theatre* (Cambridge: Cambridge University Press, 2004).

Krauss, Rosalind E., *The Optical Unconscious* (Cambridge MA and London: MIT Press, 1993).

Kroll, Jack, "Placing the Living Shakespeare Before Us," *New York Times* (February 7, 1971), D1.

Kustow, Michael, *Peter Brook: A Biography* (New York: St. Martin's Press, 2005).

Lahr, John, "He That Plays the King," *The New Yorker* 83.25 (August 27, 2007).

Lakoff, George and Mark Johnson, *Philosophy in the Flesh: The Embodied Mind and Its Challenge to Western Thought* (New York: Basic Books, 1999).

Lepecki, Andre, *Exhausting Dance: Performance and the Politics of Movement* (London and New York: Routledge, 2006).

Lipking, Lawrence, "The Marginal Gloss," *Critical Inquiry* 3.4 (1977), 609–655.

Loney, Glenn, ed. *Peter Brook's Production of William Shakespeare's A Midsummer Night's Dream for The Royal Shakespeare Company: Authorized Acting Edition* (Chicago, IL: Dramatic Publishing Company and The Royal Shakespeare Company of Stratford-upon-Avon, 1974).

Lyons, Bridget Gellert, ed. *Chimes at Midnight: Orson Welles, Director*, Rutgers Films in Print (New Brunswick, NJ: Rutgers University Press, 1988).

McAuley, Gay, *Space in Performance: Making Meaning in the Theatre* (Ann Arbor, MI: University of Michigan Press, 2000).

——, *Not Magic But Work: An Ethnographic Account of a Rehearsal Process* (Manchester: Manchester University Press, 2012).

McGann, Jerome J., *The Textual Condition* (Princeton, NJ: Princeton University Press, 1991).

Mack, Gardner, "Expert Bewails Tendency to Star 'Punch' Instead of the Story," *The Washington Times* (May 29, 1915), 15.

Maguire, Laurie E., *Shakespearean Suspect Texts: the "Bad" Quartos and Their Contexts* (Cambridge: Cambridge University Press, 1996).

Manvell, Roger, *Ellen Terry* (New York: Putnam, 1968).

Marx, Ursula et al., eds. *Walter Benjamin's Archive*, trans. Esther Lewis (London and New York: Verso, 2007).

Merleau-Ponty, Maurice, *Phenomenology of Perception*, trans. Colin Smith (New York: Humanities Press, 1970).

Mink, Louis, "Everyman His Other Analyst," *Critical Inquiry* 7.4 (1981), 777–783.

Mulvey, Laura, "Visual Pleasure and Narrative Cinema," in Mulvey, *Visual and Other Pleasures* (Bloomington, IN: Indiana University Press, 1989). (Originally in *Screen* 16.3 (Autumn 1975), 6–18.)

Nelson, Robin, "Practice-as-Research: The Problem of Knowledge," *Performance Research* 11.4 (London: Taylor & Francis, 2006), 101–116.

Netz, Reviel and William Noel, *The Archimedes Codex: How a Medieval Prayer Book Is Revealing the True Genius of Antiquity's Greatest Scientist* (London: Weidenfeld & Nicholson, 2007).

Noland, Carrie, "The Human Situation on Stage: Merce Cunningham, Theodor Adorno, and the Category of Expression," *Dance Research Journal* 42.1. (Summer 2010), 46–60.

Onians, John, ed. *Sight and Insight: Essays on Art and Culture in Honor of E.H. Gombrich at 85* (London: Phaidon Press, 1993).

Palfrey, Simon and Tiffany Stern, *Shakespeare in Parts* (Oxford: Oxford University Press, 2007).

Pascoe, Judith, *The Sarah Siddons Audio Files* (Ann Arbor, MI: University of Michigan Press, 2011).

Pearce, Susan M., *On Collecting: An Investigation into Collecting in the European Tradition* (London and New York: Routledge, 1995).

Pearson, Michael and Michael Shanks, *Theatre/Archaeology* (London and New York: Routledge, 2001).

Penney, Barbara, "Staging the Dream," in *Peter Brook's Production of William Shakespeare's A Midsummer Night's Dream for The Royal Shakespeare Company: Authorized Acting Edition*, ed. Glenn Loney (Chicago: Dramatic Publishing Company and The Royal Shakespeare Company of Stratford-upon-Avon, 1974), 93–98.

Phelan, Peggy, *Unmarked: The Politics of Performance* (London and New York: Routledge, 1993).

Pitcher, John, ed. *The Winter's Tale*, Arden 3 edition (London: Methuen Drama, 2010).

Preiss, Richard, "Robert Armin Do the Police in Different Voices," in *From Performance to Print in Shakespeare's England*, ed. Peter Holland and Stephen Orgel (Houndsmill, Basingstoke: Palgrave Macmillan, 2006), 208–230.

Ranciere, Jacques, *The Emancipated Spectator*, trans. Gregory Elliott (London and New York: Verso, 2009).

Rayner, Alice, *Ghosts: Death's Double and the Phenomena of Theatre* (Minneapolis, MN: University of Minnesota Press, 2006).

Reason, Matthew, "Archive or Memory? The Detritus of Live Performance," *New Theatre Quarterly* 19.1 (2003), 82–89.

Roach, Joseph, *Cities of the Dead: Circum-Atlantic Performance* (New York: Columbia University Press, 1996).

Rokem, Freddie, *Philosophers and Thespians: Thinking Performance* (Redwood City, CA: Stanford University Press, 2010).

Rubery, Matthew, ed. *Audiobooks, Literature and Sound Studies* (London: Routledge, 2011).

Rutter, Carol Chillington, *Shakespeare's Lost Boys on Stage and Screen* (London and New York: Routledge, 2007).

Schechner, Richard, *Between Theatre and Anthropology* (Philadelphia, PA: University of Pennsylvania Press, 1985).

Schneider, Rebecca, *Performance Remains: Art and War in Times of Theatrical Reenactment* (London and New York: Routledge, 2011).

——, "Performance Remains Again," in *Archaeologies of Presence: Art, Performance and the Persistence of Being*, ed. Gabriella Giannachi, with Nick Kaye and Michael Shanks (London and New York: Routledge, 2012), 64–81.

Scott, Joan W., "Storytelling." Forum: Holberg Prize Symposium on Doing Decentered History. *History and Theory* 50 (May 2011), 203–209.

Selbourne, David, *The Making of A Midsummer Night's Dream: An Eye-Witness Account of Peter Brook's Production From First Rehearsal to First Night* (London: Methuen, 1982).

The Shakespeare Sessions. DVD (Working Arts Library, Denver Center for the Performing Arts, Applause Theatre and Cinema Books, n.d.).

Shelton, Anthony, "Cabinets of Transgression: Renaissance Collections and the Incorporation of the New World," in *The Cultures of Collecting*, ed. John Elsner and Roger Cardinal (Cambridge, MA: Harvard University Press, 1994), 177–203.

Sher, Antony, *The Year of the King: An Actor's Diary and Sketchbook* (London: Chatto and Windus, 1985).

——, "The Fool in *King Lear*," in *Players 2*, ed. Russell Jackson and Robert Smallwood (Cambridge: Cambridge University Press, 1988), 151–166.

——, *Characters, Paintings, Drawings, Sketches* (London: Nick Hern Books, 1989).

——, *Beside Myself: An Autobiography* (London: Hutchinson, 2001).

Sherman, William H., *Used Books: Marking Readers in Renaissance England* (Philadelphia, PA: University of Pennsylvania Press, 2008).

Sklar, Deidre, "Can Bodylore Be Brought to Its Senses?," *Journal of American Folklore* 107.423 (1994), 9–22.

Smith, Bruce R. "Ragging *Twelfth Night* 1602, 1996, 2002–03," in *A Companion to Shakespeare and Performance*, ed. Barbara Hodgdon and W.B. Worthen (Oxford: Blackwell Publishing, 2005), 57–78.

Spiecker, Sven, *The Big Archive: Art From Bureaucracy* (Cambridge, MA: MIT Press, 2008).

Stafford, Barbara Maria, *Visual Analogy: Consciousness as the Art of Connecting* (Cambridge, MA: MIT Press, 1999).

Staiger, Janet, "Cabinets of Transgression: Collecting and Arranging Hollywood Images," *Participations* 1.3 (February 2005), 1–33.

Stanislavski, Konstantin, *An Actor's Work on a Role*, trans. and ed. Jean Benedetti (London and New York: Routledge, 2010).

States, Bert O., *Great Reckonings in Little Rooms: On the Phenomenology of Theater* (Berkeley, CA: University of California Press, 1985).

Steedman, Carolyn, *Dust: The Archive and Cultural History* (New Brunswick, NJ: Rutgers University Press, 2002).

Stern, Tiffany, "Actors and Parts," in *The Oxford Handbook to Early Modern Theatre*, ed. Richard Dutton (Oxford University Press, 2009).

Swann, Marjorie, *Curiosities and Texts: The Culture of Collecting in Early Modern England* (Philadelphia, PA: University of Pennsylvania Press, 2001).

Tarkovsky, Andrei, *Sculpting in Time: Reflections on the Cinema*, trans. Kitty Hunter-Blair (London: Bodley Head, 1986).

Taylor, John, *Records of My Life* (New York: J. & J. Harper, 1833) (full text available online).

Terry, Ellen, *The Story of My Life: Recollections and Reflections* (New York: McClure Co., 1908).

——, *Ellen Terry's Memoirs* (New York: Putnam's Sons, 1932).

——, *Four Lectures on Shakespeare*, ed. and with an introduction by Christopher St John (London: Hopkinson, 1932).

Toporkov, Vasili, *Stanislavski in Rehearsal*, trans. and intro. Jean Benedetti (London: Methuen, 2001).

Turkle, Sherry, *Evocative Objects: Things to Think With* (Cambridge, MA: MIT Press, 2007).

Vale-Humphreys, Marian, *Autograph Book, 1932–1972*. Shakespeare Centre Library.

Wild, Jennifer, "The Length of a Wide Highway: On the Archive, the (Electronic) Marketplace, and the End of a Collection," *Cinémas* 24.2–3, special issue L'attrait de l'archive (Summer 2014): 165–187.

Windsor, John, "Identity Parades," in *The Cultures of Collecting*, ed. John Elsner and Roger Cardinal (Cambridge, MA: Harvard University Press, 1994), 49–67.

Wittkower, D.E., *A Preliminary Phenomenology of the Audio Book* (London and New York: Routledge, 2011).

Worthen, W.B., "Antigone's Bones," *The Drama Review* (*TDR*) 52.3 (2008), 10–33.

——, "Shakespeare/Performance Studies," in *The Shakespeare International Yearbook*, vol. 10 (Burlington, VT: Ashgate, 2009), 77–92.

Yates, Frances A., *The Art of Memory* (Chicago, IL and London: University of Chicago Press, 1966).

Yumibe, Joshua, *Moving Color: Early Film, Mass Culture and Modernism* (New Brunswick, NJ and London: Rutgers University Press, 2012).

INDEX